AND THEN
YOU WERE GONE

AND THEN
YOU WERE GONE

RESTORING A BROKEN HEART
AFTER PREGNANCY LOSS

BECKY AVELLA

Blue Azalea Press (3313 W. Cherry Lane #126, Meridian, Idaho 83642) functions only as book publisher. As such, the ultimate design, content, editorial accuracy, and views expressed or implied in this work are those of the author.

Unless otherwise noted, all Scriptures are taken from the *Holy Bible, New International Version*®, *NIV*®. Copyright © 1973, 1978, 1984 by Biblica, Inc.™ Used by permission of Zondervan. All rights reserved worldwide. WWW.ZONDERVAN.COM

Scripture quotations marked NLT are taken from the Holy Bible, New Living Translation, copyright © 1996. Used by permission of Tyndale House Publishers, Inc., Wheaton, Illinois 60189. All rights reserved.

Scripture references marked KJV are taken from the *King James Version* of the Bible.

Scripture quotations marked NKJV are taken from the New King James Version®. Copyright © 1982 by Thomas Nelson, Inc. Used by permission. All rights reserved.

Scripture quotations marked THE MESSAGE are taken from *The Message* by Eugene H. Peterson, copyright © 1993, 1994, 1995, 1996, 2000, 2001, 2002. Used by permission of NavPress Publishing Group. All rights reserved.

Scripture quotations marked AMP are taken from the Amplified Bible, Copyright © 1954, 1958, 1962, 1964, 1965, 1987 by The Lockman Foundation. Used by permission.

ISBN-13: 978-1499102819
ISBN-10: 149910281X
Library of Congress Catalog Card Number: 2009909169

He heals the brokenhearted and binds up their wounds.

—Ps. 147:3

CONTENTS

ACKNOWLEDGMENTS

Daiquiri Fouch: My faithful friend who told me to write this book and believed I could. You carried my burdens and provided a shoulder to cry on when I needed it the most. Your belief in me is an amazing gift, and your vision for this book existed long before its conception. It would not have become a reality without you.

Jennifer Hilty-Jones: You took to heart the command to "mourn with those who mourn." Your example of strength and dependence on the Lord through my trial was my inspiration. I love seeing how God has made beauty from the ashes of your life.

Mom and Dad: My cheerleaders. I wouldn't have had the confidence to share my testimony without your encouragement and prayers. Dad, thank you for giving me a love for words and for your tireless editing help. This is a better book because of the time and talent you poured into the editing process.

Dr. Terry Pape: My soul's tour guide. Thank you for teaching me to grieve and helping me to see where God wanted to heal.

Dr. Timothy West: You will never know how your prayers and presence were a gift to us. You were present at the most joyful moments of my life, the birth of Karissa and Amy, and a quiet comfort during my worst nightmares. Thank you. Thank you for not giving up on us and for helping us push through to our miracle.

Cheryl, Mindy, Jeanine, Cynthia, Julie, Randi, Monique, Noreen, Colleen, Ann, Angie, Mary Ellen, Marisa, Sarah, Amanda, Lisa, Gayla, Bonnie, Tonia, and Beth: Women who have also walked this painful journey. Thank you for comforting me just as you were also comforted. God used your example and words in my healing. Your understanding and empathy were priceless. Seeing how you chose joy instead of bitterness was a testimony to me. I pray this book will be a comfort to hurting women as all of you were to me.

The Women of Calvary Chapel Boise: My sisters. You allowed me to be weak and cry so many times. Thank you for your prayers and love. Thank you for using God's Word to teach me and to minister to me.

My Cherished Family and Friends: Thank you for the servants you were to our family in our time of need. The meals, the hugs, the tears, the words of love, and your prayers carried us through. Jesus loved us through all of you.

Karissa and Amy: My joy. Thank you for giving me a reason to smile through my tears. Every good and perfect gift is from the Father above, and I am eternally grateful He blessed me with both of you. Thank you for continually reminding me to look to Heaven and to remember that it is a wonderful place. You'll never know how much your childlike wisdom and sweetness ministered to me.

David, Micah, James, and Sarah: My angels. You have gone ahead of me to Heaven and have given me a reason to hope and long for eternity. Your lives were short, but I am confident they will serve a great purpose. I am so thankful that we are only separated for a time. My heart aches for the time when I will be with you again.

Pat: My hero. I could never have survived all of this without your tenderness and strength. Everyday you prove to me again that you truly are my knight in shining armor. You are my best friend, and I am so thankful for the ways you allowed me to lean on you in my hurt. Thank you for believing I could write this.

Jesus: The Healer of Broken Hearts, I thank you above all else. Without you, Lord, I never would have survived the hurt. Please use this book to point other women to You so they can know Your love and healing, too. I love You.

CHAPTER 1

MY STORY

I DIDN'T KNOW that morning when I woke up this was going to be the day that changed my life forever. Life is like that; tragedy and grief can smack you upside the head when you are least expecting it, leaving you beat up from the paralyzing shock.

It was a beautiful Tuesday morning in May, and I was excited. I was five months pregnant with our third child, and today was ultrasound day. I always get so excited for the ultrasounds. I'm too impatient to wait until their delivery to find out the sex of my children, so I couldn't wait to peek. I kissed my husband, Pat, goodbye as he left for work and told him I'd meet him at the doctor's office in a couple hours for our appointment. I remember saying, "I'm so excited. Today feels like Christmas."

I was positive we were going to have a son. We already had Karissa and Amy, our two beautiful little girls. A son would make our family complete.

I got the girls dressed and we drove into the parking lot just as Pat arrived. What a beautiful spring day! Pat carried Amy, and I held Karissa's hand as she skipped into the doctor's office. I felt such contentment sitting in the waiting room. I could see other pregnant moms smiling at my two cute little girls.

As we entered the ultrasound room, I handed the tech my videotape and told her we wanted to see a baby boy on the TV screen. She laughed and began the scan. Within minutes, all of the joy of that spring day disappeared. I was familiar enough with ultrasounds to know what should be on the screen. The tech remained quiet, and I could sense her tension. Then she began to scan the heart. Instead of peaks and valleys, the screen remained blank. Instead of the sound of the ultra-fast beating of a baby's heart, there was silence. She kept scanning and scanning and still more silence. She set down the wand and bravely said, "I need to step outside and speak with your doctor for a minute. I'll be right back." My heart broke at that moment. I knew.

I delivered our baby boy three days later in the hospital. He was seven inches long and weighed less than half a pound. We named him David Patrick Avella. David meaning "beloved," and Patrick after his daddy, so the world would know he was our beloved son. The nurses wrapped him in a quilt and put a blue hat on him, and I held him to my chest. I had been dreaming about having him sleep on my chest. I remember crying, "My baby boy. My baby boy."

When I was discharged from the hospital, they wheeled me away in a wheelchair. Leaving David's body in that room was the hardest thing I have ever done. I am still haunted at times by the memory.

The following months were filled with grief, depression, and healing. God was close to me. My friends and family surrounded me with love and support. We planted a tree in our backyard in remembrance of David. I thanked God for getting us through such a hard trial.

Trying Again

Throughout the summer, I knew I wanted another baby. I shared with my friends how much I longed to try again, but I knew my husband wasn't on the same page. He seemed content to put our loss behind us and move on, thankful for the two children we had. I began to pray that God would soften Pat's heart and make him desire another baby, too. I waited God to work to make Pat ready.

In September, Pat was ready. I praised God! What a beautiful thing He had done. I conceived quickly and I rejoiced that I was pregnant again before David's due date on October 10th. Our baby would come in June. How perfect! My mom and dad would be finished teaching for the school year and would be able to come and help. I couldn't have planned it better. I kept looking at that positive pregnancy test, hopeful again for the first time.

One week later, I began to spot, then came a full-blown period. It was all over, again!

I couldn't understand what was happening. My first two pregnancies were so easy and perfect. I was convinced I was made to have babies. Why was my body failing me now?

I went to visit my doctor for some direction. His opinion was that these two losses were unrelated. He told me early miscarriages like mine are very common. Many women have early miscarriages and don't even know they have miscarried. They are a little late with or having their period, and then have a slightly harder or longer period. I asked him about conceiving again, and he didn't see any reason why we shouldn't be able to try again soon.

We conceived that very month, but decided to keep it a secret until we were sure we were going to stay pregnant this time. We told our immediate family first. During prayer at Thanksgiving dinner, Pat prayed "And thank You for the baby that Becky is going to have." The table erupted with joy. The rest of our friends and family heard our news through our Christmas cards we signed, "Love, Pat, Becky, Karissa, Amy, and Baby due July 26th!"

I was excited, but reserved. I think I expected loss instead of a baby. On New Year's Day, I realized I was afraid to think of names or to make plans for the nursery. I decided I needed to spend some time in prayer asking God to forgive me for my unbelief. It felt so good to let go of the fear and to start looking expectantly and excitedly toward the future. I really believed He had blessed us with another son. That night, Pat and I sat on the girls' beds and watched them play, while we discussed plans for the nursery. We started brainstorming ideas for names.

In mid-January, I was thirteen weeks pregnant and went to visit my doctor for a routine check-up. "Well," he said, "you've made it to that point in your pregnancy where we can begin to relax a little bit. Except with your history, I'm not sure we'll ever really relax." He started listening for the baby's heartbeat. He kept listening and listening. Soon tears were streaming down my cheeks. "Don't worry," he said. "It is common not to hear the heartbeat with the Doppler. I'll let the ultrasound tech know you are coming." I tried to reassure myself as I sat waiting. We had already heard this baby's heartbeat many times. It had only been two weeks since we heard it last.

The ultrasound technician was thorough. "I'm sorry," she said, "I just can't find any cardiac activity."

I was shocked. How could this be happening again?

THE NEED FOR AN EXPLANATION

Three days later, I had a D&C procedure. It was awful. When I had delivered David, the hospital staff had treated us wonderfully. They understood that we were grieving, and helped us through the process every step of the way. We were given mementos and were allowed to hold David for as long as we needed. They gave us opportunities for closure.

This time at a surgery center, the procedure was so clinical. They put me to sleep and then woke me up. It was all over. I was empty, and I could go home.

As I recovered physically, I struggled so much with depression and a desperate need for an explanation. I put much faith in the medical community. They had to be able to tell me what was wrong. We ordered every test possible. Yet each test came back with the same result: This baby boy was normal. The parents are normal. No explanation.

TRUST ME

Many months later, Pat and I began talking about whether or not we could or would ever try again. We were both terrified, but felt compelled to try once more. In my own prayer time, I felt as if I kept hearing from the Lord, "I want you to trust me. I will not give you an assurance of the outcome. I am just asking you to trust me." We went to the elders of our church and had them lay hands on us and pray for this decision. I remember how peaceful I felt as I left that room. I remembered them praying that God would do exceedingly more than we even could imagine in the way He answered our prayers. Three weeks later, I discovered I was pregnant again.

It was important to me to do everything right this time. I wouldn't stand in front of the microwave, I put a filter on our faucet for our drinking water, and I used all natural cleaning products. I wouldn't eat hotdogs or lunchmeat. I avoided anything I could think of that might be harmful to our baby.

Many times friends and family would share with me their peace about this pregnancy and how they knew that this time God would bless us with success. I leaned on everyone's faith and expectancy, but had a difficult time believing it myself. As I sought God about my lack of faith, He continued to speak to my heart, "I will not give you an assurance of the outcome. I want you to trust me." I did trust Him, and I began to visualize how victorious we would feel in the delivery room, but January felt like a lifetime away. How could we ever make it that far?

On Tuesday morning, July 25th, we went in as a family for a quick check-up. We had scheduled a trip to visit my grandmother the following morning and wanted to reassure our minds before we left, so we could enjoy a worry-free trip. Knowing I was thirteen weeks pregnant, the same spot in my pregnancy I had been in January when we lost our third baby, made me anxious about going into the doctor's office.

Every time I entered that office, I felt like I was walking to the guillotine, but this time I was extremely nervous. The night before, I had a gruesome nightmare. In the dream, there had been blood everywhere, and I had delivered my baby stillborn. The dream shook me up and added to the stress of going into the office that day.

Once again, I found myself lying in the office with a silent Doppler going over my belly. I panicked. My doctor tried to reassure me it was early in my pregnancy, making it tricky to hear on the Doppler, but we had heard a strong heartbeat on that same Doppler only a few weeks before. I knew it was happening all over again. He left to let the ultrasound technicians know we were coming.

The ultrasound tech tried to find a heartbeat, but finally laid the wand down and said, "I'm sorry. I'll stop torturing you now." I'll never forget how Pat's whole body sagged and his head flopped back, as he said incredulously, "Again?"

That one word said it all. "Again? You told me to trust you. Again, Lord? No!"

Karissa and Amy were trying to figure out what was going on. Amy asked, "Why is Mommy crying, Daddy?" When we told them, Karissa crawled into my lap and said, "Don't be sad, Mommy. Our baby is in Heaven and Heaven is a wonderful place."

Four babies in Heaven. Four! How could that be possible?

We decided to hurry up the D&C procedure this time, so we could still go on our planned vacation the following morning. Pat felt like Grandma's house would be a good place to recover and my mom and grandma would be able to distract the girls with fun. Our appointment had been at 9 A.M. By four in the afternoon, I was in surgery. By six the next morning we were on the road. It happened so fast I didn't have time to do anything except be in shock.

For a month and a half, I kept it together. We did a lot of traveling and I just wouldn't allow myself to feel anything. Then one day I ran out of strength. The day before I had been fine; the next day I couldn't function. I had never felt such despair.

GOD IS FAITHFUL

After all this grief and heartache, I am still able to proclaim that God is good, God is faithful, and God does heal.

My road to recovery and healing physically, mentally, emotionally, and spiritually, has not been easy and is not over. My healing is and will continue to be a process. I have continually struggled with depression, with fear, and with the belief that God is punishing me. I have drawn near to God at times, and at other times I have run away to lick my wounds. Through it all, He has called to me gently, saying, "Becky, I love you. I will never leave you nor forsake you. And I am willing to heal you if you'll let me."

I do not tell my story to make you sad, though it is a sad story. I am not writing this to prepare you for more losses in your future. Every journey is different. If you have experienced first miscarriage, this book is not a warning that more are coming.

I tell my story because I want you to know I have been there. I know the helpless feeling of bleeding and not being able to stop it. I know the shock and emptiness after a D&C procedure. I know what it is like to hold your baby who is no longer alive. My heart breaks for you because my own heart was broken. I've been to the place where your sadness feels unbearable and the hole in your heart seems impossible to mend.

More than anything, I tell it because this sad story has a happy ending. It begins with brokenness and ends with joy.

Throughout all four of my losses, God has sent me other women who have also dealt with pregnancy loss. All of them mysteriously showed up just when I needed them. Even if they didn't have any words for me, knowing they had felt the same pain and emptiness, both spiritually and physically, has helped so much. After experiencing this type of comfort, I want to comfort others. It is my prayer that this book will stand in my place alongside those of you who are grieving the terrible loss of a baby, as a girlfriend would, loving you and comforting you, and pointing you to Jesus.

Every pregnancy loss is different. Each of my losses was different. This book will share with you the biblical and practical wisdom that continues to lead to my healing, but I do not expect that your journey will be the same as mine, or that your loss was the same. The answer to healing is the same, however: Seek Jesus. Jesus is the Great Physician and He can and will heal your broken heart.

CHAPTER 2

WHERE ARE YOU?

DRAWING NEAR TO GOD FOR HEALING

Draw near to God and He will draw near to you.

—Js. 4:8 NKJV

THAT BEAUTIFUL MAY day had turned into a nightmare. My baby's heart had stopped beating. It just couldn't be possible.

The doctor's nurse led Karissa and Amy away to play and left Pat and me alone, waiting for the doctor. I sat on the examination table, aware of the paper sticking to my sweaty legs. Staring ahead, the tears streamed down my face, and I didn't try to stop them. A strong desire to run away overcame me. If I could run away, I might be able to outrun this nightmare.

Turning to the right, I remember physically feeling God's presence preventing me from bolting. I turned to the left and again I felt His presence holding me. In my heart, I heard Him say, "Becky, I'm to your left. I'm to your right. I will be anywhere you try to run from me. Run to me, not away from me."

That next morning I wrote this in my prayer journal:

May 18

Father,

Where can I go from Your Spirit? Or where can I flee from Your presence? If I ascend into Heaven, You are there: If I make my bed in hell, behold, You are there. If I take the wings of the morning, and dwell in the uttermost parts of the sea, even there Your hand shall lead me, and Your right hand shall hold me.

—Ps. 139:7-10 NKJV

Your grace surrounds me. If I turn to the right or to the left, You are there. My heart is broken, yet I find joy in knowing You haven't forsaken me. I don't understand why You took my baby from me. I trust in You. I need You.

I didn't write in my journal again for a month. Numb with grief, I couldn't pray, read, or study the Bible. My mind blurred everything I read. Reading the same paragraph over and over again, I eventually gave up. Despite my inability to *do* anything, God was there and was speaking to me. All I could do was lean on Him.

Although I couldn't make the spiritual effort I thought I was supposed to make to please God, it became a sweet time of rest. I was weak and had nothing to offer, so I leaned on Him and He carried me.

Sadly, I did not remain in this state of rest. I became convinced, I was somehow failing God and He was angry and punishing me. The lies of the Enemy led to discouragement and despair. Distracted from my relationship with the Lord, I drifted, and often ran away to hide. I was afraid to get close to Him, afraid of what He would do next. I craved His comfort, but I became a ping-pong ball, bouncing from His arms to my own self-imposed distance.

I also wanted to pull away from other people. Church was an almost unbearable place to be. Each week I would think, "I'm fine today," but the desire to leave the building would hit immediately upon entering. Week after week I tried to "be strong this time" and would make myself sit in the sanctuary. As worship began, the music stirred my emotions, leaving me vulnerable, and the tears would inevitably start falling. I thought, *I have to get out of here or I'm going to start bawling,* but I realized walking out would allow everyone to see I had been crying. If I stayed, I wouldn't be able to keep from sobbing and causing a scene. I was trapped. If I did choose to leave the sanctuary, I would wander around until the service ended, trying to get myself under control and presentable before anyone could see me.

Picking up Karissa and Amy from their classes, I would run into well meaning people who were unaware of the situation. They would look at me with a quizzical look and innocently ask, "When are you due?" I felt awful explaining everything, watching those sweet people become mortified as they realized their question had hurt me.

This struggle continued for months. It was so painful and embarrassing to be at church, and there were constant reminders of my loss. Churches are full of pregnant women and babies. One service ended for me when I opened a bulletin and read an advertisement for the upcoming Father/Son campout.

However, knowing I needed to at church by God's strength, I continued to show up at services and Bible studies week after week. I was constantly embarrassed by my weakness. Telling myself, *I'm not going to cry this time*, didn't work. I always ended up in tears. I hated being so emotional publicly, but I didn't know how to stop it.

LIKE ENOCH

In one of the weekly Bible studies I read about Enoch. The story of this simple Bible character became a turning point for me in my healing process.

I wasn't consciously deciding to pull away from God, but I continued to do it out of fear. Desperate to please and appease Him, I needed to figure out how to make God happy with me again. Pointing me to the story of Enoch was His answer to that desperation.

After the Bible study, I wrote this in my prayer journal:

January 1

Dear Father,
I am so thankful for this opportunity to be in Your presence,
yet it is a struggle for me. I've drifted and have found myself in
spiritual fog. I feel so far away from You, and it is not a place
I want to stay. Please help me. Bring me back. Revive me. I've
been so afraid that I am displeasing You. I have been running
away from You, when what pleases You is for us to walk with
You like Enoch.

Enoch walked with God; then he was no more, because God
took him away.

—Gen. 5:24

By faith Enoch was taken from this life, so that he did not experience death; he could not be found, because God had taken him
away. For before he was taken, he was commended as one who
pleased God.

—Heb. 11:5

Enoch is hardly mentioned in the Bible, yet he is included in
the list of heroes of the faith found in Hebrews 11. What was it
that pleased God about Enoch? The Bible says, "Enoch walked
with God." That's it?

Enoch had a relationship with the Lord that was so sweet to
God, He reached down and took Enoch to be with Him. There is
no mention of great works or miracles done, no huge following of
disciples, no temples built, nothing, just that he walked with God
and that pleased God.

It became clear to me that if I wanted to truly please God, running away was the worst possible decision. Instead of retreating in
fear, I needed to draw near Him in order to heal.

Walking with the Lord. Drawing near to Him in faith. Abiding
in Him. Trusting Him. Talking with Him. Listening to Him. Loving
Him. Believing the truth about Him. Allowing Him to heal and
change me. This pleases the Lord. I wanted to be like Enoch because
Enoch was "commended as one who pleased God" (Heb. 11:5).

Who Was I Fooling?

While hiding, I should have known God knew exactly where I was; He was waiting for me to come to Him. I'm reminded of Adam in the Garden of Eden after he fell into temptation. He ran and hid from the Lord.

> And they heard the sound of the LORD God walking in the garden in the cool of the day, and Adam and his wife hid themselves from the presence of the LORD God among the trees of the garden. Then the LORD God called to Adam and said to him, "Where are you?"
> —Gen. 3:8-9 NKJV

Each time I read this passage of scripture, I'm struck by how silly it was for Adam and Eve to hide (as if anyone *can* hide from God). But I've tried to many times. When God asked Adam, "Where are you?" God didn't need help finding him. The question was for Adam's benefit. "Where have you gone, Adam? Why are you hiding from me?"

Each time I've drawn away from the Lord, He has called out, "Where are you, Becky?" He loves me and woos me back each time I stray. Everything I need is in His hands. He alone could heal my wounded heart, but I had to choose to come out of hiding and allow him to do so.

Acquainted with Grief

> He is despised and rejected by men, a Man of sorrows and acquainted with grief.
> —Isa. 53:3 NKJV

I came to Him in the midst of my sorrow instead of running away. I came to the One who can really understand.

No one understands grief as Jesus does. The Bible teaches that He is acquainted with grief. In the Garden of Gethsemane, Jesus said, "My soul is overwhelmed with sorrow to the point of death" (Matt. 26:38). On the cross, He cried out, "My God, my God, why have you forsaken me?" (Matt. 27:46). We can never understand the depth of Jesus' grief, yet He understands ours. Hebrews 4:15 says, "For we do not have a High Priest who cannot sympathize with our weaknesses, but was in all *points* tempted as *we are*, *yet* without sin (NKJV)." There is no aspect of our lives in which Jesus cannot sympathize with us. He knows.

My favorite of the classic *Chronicles of Narnia* series by C.S. Lewis is *The Magician's Nephew*. It is my favorite primarily because of the following scene. The main character in the book, a little boy named Digory, approaches the lion, Aslan, who represents Jesus. Digory asks Aslan to heal his mother of an illness that is killing her.

What happens next surprises Digory and spoke to me in my grieving:

> For the tawny face was bent down near his own and (wonder of wonders) great shining tears stood in the Lion's eyes. They were such big, bright tears compared with Digory's own that for a moment he felt as if the Lion must really be sorrier about his Mother than he was himself.
>
> "My son, my son," said Aslan. "I know. Grief is great. Only you and I in this land know that yet. Let us be good to one another."[1]

Why would we pull away from Jesus, when He above all others can empathize with our pain? He knows our grief better than we know it ourselves. He empathizes with our pain, and fills us up with Himself so we can endure it.

JARS OF CLAY

> But we have this treasure in jars of clay to show that this all-surpassing power is from God and not from us. We are hard pressed on every side, but not crushed; perplexed, but not in despair; persecuted, but not abandoned; struck down, but not destroyed.
> —2 Cor. 4:7-9

An empty clay jar. What a perfect description of how I felt about myself. Empty. Easily shattered. It is hard to describe to someone who has never experienced it, but the feeling of emptiness one feels after being full of life during pregnancy, and then losing that life, is overwhelming. I felt purposeless, aimless, and empty, but God was rescuing me.

When we choose to draw near to God in that state of emptiness, we are filled. On our own, we are easily shattered. As soon as the pressures of this world outweigh the pressure inside, all of the adjectives above fit us: crushed, full of despair, abandoned, destroyed. On the flip side, when we feel stronger than the pressure outside, we cannot be crushed or destroyed. We are called to draw near to God when we grieve because without Him, we will be destroyed.

I am still an empty clay jar without Him, but by drawing near to Him, He, along with all of His resources, draws near to me and strengthens me by His power. It isn't something I can accomplish on my own; He fills my empty vessel with Himself.

CAN I HAVE A PIECE OF PEACE, PLEASE?

Remain in me, and I will remain in you. No branch can bear fruit by itself; it must remain in the vine. Neither can you bear fruit unless you remain in me. I am the vine; you are the branches. If a man remains in me and I in him, he will bear much fruit; apart from me you can do nothing.

—John 15:4-5

But the fruit of the Spirit is love, joy, peace, patience, kindness, goodness, faithfulness, gentleness and self-control.

—Gal. 5:22-23

During another Bible study, we talked about how people approach God seeking His blessings, when what they really want and need is Him. They come to Him, asking for strength or peace to make it through something, as if God were up in Heaven passing out slices of pie. "Here's a slice of strength. Here's some love, and I'll give you a nice, big hunk of joy for tomorrow."

He doesn't do that. Instead, He gives us Himself. He *is* joy. He *is* peace. He *is* love. These are aspects of His nature. When we need strength, we are to run to Him and He will *be* our strength. I'm not to say, "Sir, may I have a piece of peace, please?" I am to run to Him, acknowledging my lack of peace and my need for more of Him.

I learned to seek Him, and not some slice of blessing to overcome the loss of my babies. By drawing near, God didn't pass out the ingredients I needed to get well and to recover from the losses and pain. He didn't say, "Here, take this pill and move on." By drawing near to Him, He drew near to me. He didn't give me a remedy. He *was* my remedy.

As my personal failures flooded in to condemn me, instead of pulling away again, I had to learn the difference between condemnation and conviction. Whose voice is it that says, "How could you pray today? Look at how you yelled at your kids! You need to clean up your act before you try to pray." I began to identify this voice as the condemnation of Satan the Accuser. His voice sent me running in shame, away from God's healing.

In contrast, the Holy Spirit's voice of conviction revealed areas of my heart that God wanted to work on or heal. He is gentle, but He tells the truth. His voice sent me falling at God's feet in repentance, seeking Him for forgiveness and healing.

Recognizing my failures became a measuring stick to judge where I was in my relationship with the Lord. Was I lacking peace? Was I being impatient? Was I lacking self-control? Then it was time to repent and once again draw near to God, instead of hiding and being paralyzed by condemnation.

Only God Can Heal Me

Woe to those who go down to Egypt for help, who rely on horses, who trust in the multitude of their chariots and in the great strength of their horsemen, but do not look to the Holy One of Israel, or seek help from the LORD.

—Isa. 31:1

Several sources told me where to find help. The miscarriage literature assured me time would heal me. The pamphlets said it would take at least a year to get over the pain. People told me that having another baby would heal me. I thought my antidepressants would make me all better. All three might make me feel better, but they were lacking the power to truly heal my wound.

Satan seduces us away from the Lord, distracting us with worldly wisdom because he has a different objective than our healing; He wants to destroy you and me. He is fully aware that running to Jesus leads to healing.

I had to understand that God would heal me, not time. God would heal me, not another baby. God would heal me, not medication. He may use time and another baby and modern medicine as part of His planned work, but He would do the work.

It is foolish to go to any other source, when Hebrews 4:16 says to "approach the throne of grace with confidence, so that we may receive mercy and find grace to help us in our time of need." The great power that created all that exists, that conquered death, that raised Christ from the dead, is the same power along with all of the resources of Heaven, that are mine through Christ when I draw near to Him. Where else should I run?

There is no Bible verse that says, "God helps those who help themselves." Most Americans believe it is in there somewhere because it is a cultural tradition, yet the truth is that God helps those who run to Him in weakness, and who rely upon His grace.

He also places us in a spiritual family, so we can be helped by each other. Hebrews 10:25 says, "Let us not give up meeting together, as some are in the habit of doing, but let us encourage one another—and all the more as you see the Day approaching."

As difficult as it was to control my emotions while at church, had I been able to stop the flow of emotion or hide my pain, I would have robbed other believers of an opportunity to use their gifts to minister to me.

I was amazed how many times God lined up specific people to minister to me during those times I struggled to be at church. When I left the sanctuary, a woman who had also miscarried in the past would "magically" appear to pray with me. When I felt alone and emotional, someone would hug me. When I needed a word from the Lord, someone would read Scripture that spoke directly to my heart. When I was in Bible study, people said things they didn't know were meant for me. I experienced the work of the Spirit through the love, prayers, hugs, and words of prophecy and wisdom that came from the flesh and blood people in my church family. I attend a large church, but it became small as people poured out love on me.

Some of the best comfort came from women who had been there; They could minister in a way no one else could. After she read 2 Corinthians 1:3-5, my friend, Jeanine, began praying for an opportunity to comfort someone else in the way she had been comforted when she miscarried. If I had run away from church and fellowship, I would not have been a part of that prayer being answered. It feels good to be used by the Lord. When we are weak, we allow others the privilege of being used by the Lord in our circumstance.

My pastor has shared his humorous but true belief that when Christians go off on their own they "get weird." We need each other. As we draw near to God, He often sends us to our spiritual family for some love and comfort. Don't run away.

WILLING TO HEAL

I was raised on the music of Don Francisco. His gift for putting God's heart and words to music ministers to my soul in a way no other musician has ever been able to do. Once again, God used Don's music to comfort me during this time of grieving. The song "Willing to Heal" from the album *The Power*, depicts the story of the leper who came to Jesus for healing. In the song, the man throws himself at Jesus' feet and cries out:

Lord, if You're willing,
I know that You can
Make me as clean as a natural man
I know you can do it, deep down in my soul

Oh Lord, if You're willing,
Lord, please make me whole

Jesus simply says, "I'm willing" and then heals him. The chorus of the song is this:

I'm willing to help you,
I'm willing to heal
I've born all your sufferings,
I know how you feel
Your pain can be ended, My power is real
I will not deny you, I'm willing to heal[2]

This is the same Jesus who looks at our battered and broken hearts with compassion and says, "I'm willing to heal you." Draw near to him in your weakness and let that healing begin.

Dear Father,

Help me to draw near to You in this time of grief. Do not allow me to run away. Thank You for loving my soul and for calling me to You when I do run. I know I cannot hide from You.

I am so thankful Jesus sympathizes with my pain and weakness. Show me how to walk with You and to lean on You. Your Word says to come boldly into Your throne room of grace when we need help. My heart is broken, and I need the healing only You can provide.

Forgive me for the times I turn to my own wisdom or the wisdom of this world to heal me. Prevent me from running from fellow believers. Thank You for providing a spiritual family to comfort me.

Your Word also says you are willing to heal. I seek You for that healing. I love You!

In Jesus' Name I pray,
Amen

CHAPTER 3

ENTERING THE DARKNESS

ALLOWING YOURSELF TO GRIEVE

There is a time for everything, and a season for every activity
under Heaven:
> A time to be born and a time to die,
> A time to plant and a time to uproot,
> A time to kill and a time to heal,
> A time to tear down and a time to build,
> A time to weep and a time to laugh,
> A time to mourn and a time to dance.
>
> —Eccles. 3:1-4

THE DEATHS OF my grandfathers were my only previous experiences with grief. Losing Grandpa and Papa broke my heart, but those losses didn't prepare me for the intensity of grieving the losses of my own babies.

Up to this point, my life had been idyllic. After a happy and memorable childhood, I was living my dream of being a stay-at-home mom with beautiful kids and a great marriage. I didn't see the staggering blow of tragedy coming.

This was a boxing match I never signed up to fight. The first miscarriage knocked me flat. I jumped back up quickly, afraid to stay down long. I had enough energy to get back up again and keep fighting. I wasn't going to allow the grief to get me. Besides,

I clung desperately to the hope of another baby. Another baby, I reasoned, would make this nightmare go away. Blow after blow came as I endured three more pregnancy losses. It became harder and harder to get back up again, until one day I had no fight left in me. I was knocked out, completely unable to fight grief any more. I felt defeated, and I sank into the dark night of the soul.

As I fought grief, I remember telling friends it felt as if I was treading water. I was barely able to keep my head up. I knew that if I got tired enough, I would sink into sorrow and drown in it. I ran from grief, hoping to get away from it, but I have learned like many before me that grief may be delayed, but it cannot be denied. I hit a wall and had to turn and face the Valley of the Shadow of Death.

My human nature was afraid of what I might find in that valley and wanted to avoid it at all costs. God intended to carry me through the darkness instead of allowing me to run from it, but there was another element of my human nature that compelled me to fight my grief: pride.

I knew many people were watching me to see how I would react to my losses. I imagined them wondering, *Will this shake her faith? Is she going to lose it? Will she get angry with God? How is she going to respond?* I felt immense pressure to perform properly, and I put on an appearance contrary to what was real. I thought it was my responsibility to model complete acceptance of God's will and to be a pillar of Christian strength.

I wanted to be like the models of faith that I looked up to, women like Corrie ten Boom and Elisabeth Elliot. I mistakenly thought fighting grief was the way to do it. I saw each of my miscarriages as a test to pass. I imagined God looking down from Heaven, waiting to see how I was going to perform. I believed the lie that if I truly allowed myself to grieve, I would fail Him. I stayed strong, praised God, and held it together the best that I could for a time. When I finally fell apart, I thought, *Well, I failed. I couldn't pass the test after all.* Instead, I found a compassionate God saying to me, "Now we are getting somewhere. I've been waiting for you to come to me." In 2 Corinthians 12:9 Paul writes of a valuable lesson he learned as he grew in his relationship with the Lord, "But he said to me, 'My grace is sufficient for you, for my power is made perfect in weakness.' Therefore I will boast all the more gladly about my weaknesses, so that Christ's power may rest on me." Yes, grief is painful. Yes, it leaves us weak and helpless. Yes, it is scary to face it. But grieving must be done.

After finally submitting to the grief process, I was like a shipwrecked body on the sand, as wave after wave of sorrow crashed over me. I experienced deeper pain then I ever imagined, but also compassion beyond my previous ability to comprehend. Grieving was essential to my healing. Grieving purged and cleansed my soul, so I could heal properly. As painful as it was, I needed to enter this season of weeping and mourning, so I could laugh and dance again.

Fear and pride are not the only motivations that cause a woman to avoid grief after a miscarriage. Sometimes, women feel their experience isn't bad enough to merit grief. It appears to be human nature to try to measure the extent of loss. This is especially true in response to a miscarriage. Whenever I hear of a miscarriage I even find myself asking, "Oh, how far along was she?" People comfort themselves when faced with the ugliness of a miscarriage by saying things like, "Oh well, at least she wasn't very far along." They may think, *At least she already has some children.*

In the book, *A Grace Disguised: How the Soul Grows Through Loss*, Dr. Jerry Sittser discusses the problem of trying to measure grief. He identifies the extremes people often go to in "quantifying losses." They are either "deprived of the validation they need to identify and experience the loss for the bad thing it is," or they, "convince themselves that no one has suffered as much as they have," and end up with "a strange kind of pleasure in their misery."[1]

None of these are biblically sound reasons for delaying grief. The Bible teaches there is a season to grieve. After any miscarriage, a woman receives well intended but damaging messages from other people. These comments make the woman feel as if she shouldn't be sad even in the midst of her grief. It is appropriate to grieve loss of life. As Christians, we believe life begins at conception. A miscarriage is a death, a loss of life, and that life deserves to be grieved.

It doesn't matter if other people can't understand the depth of your grief. Many cannot understand because they have not experienced it. However, you know how much you hurt. Proverbs 14:10 says, "Each heart knows its own bitterness, and no one else can share its joy." You can't wait for others to give you permission to grieve. You must allow yourself to grieve, whether this is your first miscarriage or your seventh. You must allow yourself to grieve if you were one week along in your pregnancy or eight months. After experiencing one miscarriage, someone reading this book may think, *I shouldn't feel so sad. At least I haven't gone through four miscarriages like she has.* Perhaps someone who has experienced the pain of multiple miscarriages may think, *I can't stand to grieve again.* In both cases grief may be delayed, but not denied.

Allow yourself to grieve.

Don't stop tears when they come. There were times when I would begin to cry and stop myself because I thought it was inappropriate. Then there were times I would long to cry but couldn't. Tears are healing and are a gift when they are available.

One of the best ways I found to mourn the loss of my babies was to name them. It helped me to give them an identity and to remind myself that I will be reunited with them. I grieved real babies with real names that left a real hole in my heart. The names my husband and I gave our babies were not the names they would have been given if they had lived. We used their names to express our sorrow by choosing personally meaningful names.

These are the names of my babies:

David Patrick Avella
David means "Beloved" and giving him my husband's name reminded us that he is our beloved son.

Micah Avella
Micah means "Who is like our God?" I miscarried so early it was impossible to tell if this baby was a girl or a boy. Micah was

a name that would work for a girl or a boy. The meaning of the name reminded me that God is in control, there is none like Him, and I can trust Him. In my own heart, I am convinced this baby was a girl.

James Roy Avella
Both of my grandfathers are in Heaven, so I named our son after them. It is comforting to know my babies are with Grandpa Olson and Papa.

Sarah Grace Avella
From the time I let Karissa and Amy know of my pregnancy, Amy insisted this baby was a girl and she started calling her Sarah. The name grew in my heart, too. Grace reminds me of the grace Jesus has given me that will reunite me with my baby girl. Sarah means "Princess."

It is still possible to name your baby even if your miscarriage was too early to determine the sex or if your loss happened a long time ago. Many women have an instinct or a deep belief about the sex of the baby. This was the case for me with Micah. I strongly believe our baby was a girl. You can follow that instinct when choosing a name, or you can choose a name that is still meaningful but appropriate for either sex.

One of the surprising things I discovered as I allowed myself to grieve was that it wasn't just the loss of the babies I was grieving. Experiencing the death of my babies changed me forever. I will continue to heal, but I will never be the same person. I found myself entering Part B of my life, and I didn't like it. As I grieved, I also needed to mourn the loss of the old me. The old me was innocent and never had to live with sorrow as a constant companion. The old me was carefree and optimistic. Because God carried me through this dark time, the new me is a better model. Because of the work He did in me in that valley, I am a refined and more mature woman who has an expanded ability to love, feel joy, and minister effectively; sorrow is no longer my constant companion.

I also had to mourn the loss of the future as I thought it should be. Facing the future was difficult because it held shattered dreams. Pregnancy requires you to look to the future. There are plans to be made, names to give, nurseries to paint, car seats to buy, but there is also a vision of a new person and all he or she will become. When that future vision is destroyed by miscarriage, it needs to be grieved as well.

Grieving miscarriage requires facing pain. The good news is you will not grieve alone. If you belong to Jesus, you will never be forsaken. Never. There were times when I felt completely abandoned by God. However, these were emotions and feelings, not truth. The Bible promises these things:

> You keep track of all my sorrows. You have collected all my tears in your bottle. You have recorded each one in your book.
> —Ps. 56:8 NLT

> Blessed are those who mourn, for they will be comforted.
> —Matt. 5:4

> Those who sow in tears will reap with songs of joy. He who goes out weeping, carrying seed to sow, will return with songs of joy, carrying sheaves with him.
> —Ps. 126:5-6

Dear Father,

Please give me the courage to allow myself to grieve. It is a necessary process, but I am afraid to fully face the darkness. Take away my fear and carry me through the grieving that must be done.

Remove any pride tempting me to rely on my strength instead of Your sufficient grace. Be perfect in my weakness and use it to reveal to me what is in my heart, and where I require Your touch of healing.

Remind me that the little life I carried for such a short time deserves to be mourned. Show me how best to honor that gift of life and what I need to do to grieve. I am also grieving the death of dreams. Heal those areas of great disappointment and loss. Thank you for the cleansing gift of tears.

I pray this grieving will not be in vain, but will result in a greater understanding of You and Your love. Help me to emerge from this season of darkness with a heart that is healed and restored.

In Jesus' Name I pray,
Amen

CHAPTER 4

IS GOD MAD AT ME?

WONDERING IF THIS IS PUNISHMENT

FOLLOWING THE NEWS of my fourth loss, I looked at Pat and softly said, "God must be really angry with me." I meant every word. It was the only way I knew to explain why I was sitting in this same office again, hearing the same news again, knowing the tiny little body inside of me, the one that was supposed to be okay this time, had no heartbeat.

Wondering if I was being punished wasn't a new thought. After each miscarriage, I questioned my standing with God. Obsessed with figuring out which specific sins had led to God's disfavor and judgment, I'd ask, "What did I do wrong to cause this?"

Friends and family assured me, "You aren't being punished. God loves you, He wouldn't do that." Not satisfied with this "feel good" answer, I started listing and categorizing my sins. I tried to figure out which one was the worst and which one had caused each miscarriage. During subsequent pregnancies, instead of repenting and moving on every time I sinned, I prepared myself for God's judgment, and waited to hear I had lost another baby.

After the second miscarriage, I thought I had it figured out. I have a small leadership role in the women's ministry at our church, and there was a woman in our Bible study I believed I had failed. She had been struggling for years with various issues and eventually stopped coming to our study. I felt I should reach out and develop a relationship with her, but I didn't follow through because I didn't want to. I was convinced that because I had failed her, God had judged me. I was consumed by guilt and was obsessing over this failure day and night for months.

One evening I called my mom just to talk. In the course of our conversation, I confessed my guilt and fear over this relationship and my belief that this failure was tied to my miscarriages. Mom reassured me that it was not and prayed with me. The confessing, repenting, and praying made me feel such release. All those months of carrying that burden had been exhausting, and it felt so wonderful to have the burden lifted from me. I hung up the phone, thankful for forgiveness.

One week later, I was back in the doctor's office, learning of my third pregnancy loss. When the doctor estimated the day the baby died was the same day I had had my conversation with Mom, I was convinced once again of God's disfavor and judgment, as well as the connection between this failure and my pregnancy loss. I thought, *He must not love me any more.*

My mind could understand I was forgiven, but my heart couldn't accept it. I discovered I was not alone in tying my miscarriage to specific sin. Some of the women I know who have miscarried believe their miscarriage was a direct result of a past abortion. They believe God took their wanted child in exchange for the one they had aborted years before.

Was this a true assumption? Does God use miscarriage as a form of punishment? I needed answers to my questions. I needed to know if I was being punished.

As strange as it sounds, I think a part of me wanted the answer to be yes. This was not because I wanted to be guilty or estranged from God, but because I wanted a tangible solution. If losing babies was the result of a specific sin, then logically, I should be able to shape up, fix the problem, and move on with my happy, carefree life and have another baby, right? If I could do better and pay penance, maybe God and I could put this behind us. Then He would stop punishing me.

The turning point came for me during a counseling session. I told my counselor, "Intellectually, I know God loves me, but in my heart I believe He is angry with me, punishing me, and has stopped loving me." Our conversation after that statement went something like this:

> **Dr.:** So, He doesn't love you because He didn't give you what you wanted?"
>
> **Me:** No! Of course, not.
>
> **Dr.:** If you didn't give your daughters something they wanted, would it mean you didn't love them?
>
> **Me:** No, in fact many times I don't give it to them because I *do* love them.
>
> **Dr.:** Is there anything your girls could do that would make you stop loving them?

It was a simple conversation and a concept I had heard before. However, this time there was something that clicked with me. Was I accusing God of not loving me because He wasn't giving me what I wanted? This conversation led to soul searching that eventually led to answers. Those answers led to peace.

SUFFERING IS NOT SYNONYMOUS WITH PUNISHMENT

> As he went along, he saw a man blind from birth. His disciples asked him, "Rabbi, who sinned, this man or his parents, that he was born blind?"
>
> "Neither this man nor his parents sinned," said Jesus, "but this happened so that the work of God might be displayed in his life.
>
> —John 9:1-3

In my search for answers, I began with the concept of suffering. Christians have suffered throughout history. The first question needing to be answered was, "Is suffering the same as punishment?" Looking for the answer to this question in Scripture, I found the story of the blind man being healed by Jesus in John 9.

Seeing a man they knew to be blind from birth, Jesus' disciples wondered who could be blamed for his blindness. Surely, this kind of affliction must be the result of some unspeakable sin! Jesus' answer is intriguing: "This happened so the work of God might be displayed in his life" (John 9:3).

God's purpose in allowing this man's suffering was not about punishment. He had a greater purpose for it. This man, and many others, were reconciled to God as a result of his suffering. It reveals God's heart of love for this man, not God's desire to afflict him. People often view God as vindictive, doling out punishment for the worst sinners. The prideful can then look upon a suffering person with contempt and wonder what this person did to deserve their punishment. The disciples and the Pharisees did just that to the blind man. Seeing him blind, the disciples *assumed* he had done something to deserve his plight. This was the common assumption of their day. Suffering equals punishment. Punishment is a result of sin. As this newly healed man gave his testimony before them, the Pharisees condemned him saying, "'You were steeped in sin at birth; how dare you lecture us!' And they threw him out" (John 9:34).

Human pride and reasoning have perpetuated the myth that suffering is synonymous with punishment. A good God wouldn't allow a good person to suffer. Therefore, those who suffer must not be good. We all know God hates sin, so wouldn't it make sense that he would punish sin.

The Bible teaches that God does hate sin, but it also teaches that God once and for all solved the problem of our sin. When Jesus willingly gave up His life for us on the cross, He said, "It is finished." The payment was made. The work was complete and God's wrath was satisfied. The technical term is *propitiation*. Propitiation is a legal term that means one takes the penalty for someone else. When God looks at those of us who have put our faith in Christ, He sees Jesus' righteousness and not our sin. 2 Corinthians 5:21 says, "God made him who had no sin to be sin for us, so that in him we might become the righteousness of God." Because of the cross, the punishment for sins has already been given or taken. Jesus took it for us.

In Hebrews 10:11-14 we read this wonderful promise:

"Day after day every priest stands and performs his religious duties, again and again he offers the same sacrifices, which can never take away sins. But when this priest had offered for all time one sacrifice for sins, he sat down at the right hand of God. Since that time he waits for his enemies to be made his footstool, because by one sacrifice he has made perfect forever those who are being made holy."

No amount of penance or hard work can pay for our sins. It is a gift of grace. Most believers can quote the good news of Ephesians 2:8-9, but rarely live as if it is true. "For it is by grace you have been saved, through faith—and this not from yourselves, it is the gift of God—not by works, so that no one can boast."

BUT WHY DO CHRISTIANS HAVE TO SUFFER?

A huge crowd kept following him wherever he went, because they saw his miraculous signs as he healed the sick. Then Jesus took the loaves, gave thanks to God, and distributed them to the people. Afterward he did the same with the fish. And they all ate as much as they wanted.

—John 6:2, 11 NLT

On the way, Jesus told them, "Tonight all of you will desert me. For the Scriptures say, 'God will strike the Shepherd, and the sheep of the flock will be scattered.'"

—Matt. 26:31 NLT

Satisfied with the answer that suffering isn't punishment, I then wondered, *If it isn't punishment for sin, why* do *Christians suffer?* God turned the question around on me and asked in return, "What would happen if Christians *didn't* suffer?"

Immediately, I answered, "People would choose You for the wrong reasons." I was reminded of the times when Jesus was followed by a multitude in contrast with the times when He was alone. Many people followed Jesus when they were getting something from Him. When He was healing people, the crowd was so thick it was difficult to get close to Him. When He passed out food, He fed

33

more than four thousand men on one occasion and more than five thousand another time. That didn't even account for the women and children who were with them. But after His arrest, how many remained with Him? None. In His time of suffering, the Great Shepherd was deserted by His sheep.

If by choosing to follow Jesus, people were exempt from the trials of this life along with the heartache and pain they bring, no one would choose Him for Him. They would choose Him as a "Get Out of Jail Free" card. People would ask, "You mean if I become a Christian I will never get sick, never lose a loved one, and I will have abundant material blessings that never run out? Sign me up for that deal!"

God desires the relationship with us that we were designed to have. Is it truly love if we are only after what He can "gimmee"? Is it truly love if we choose Him because we want our punishment to stop, so we finally, grudgingly cry "Uncle"? God loves us and desires true love in return from His children. One of the reasons God allows us to suffer along with this fallen world is to ensure that our love for Him is genuine, but that isn't the only reason. Another reason is that He loves this fallen world and wants us to be effective in our ministry to it.

THE GIFT OF A TESTIMONY

Praise be to the God and Father of our Lord Jesus Christ, the Father of compassion and the God of all comfort, who comforts us in all our troubles, so that we can comfort those in any trouble with the comfort we ourselves have received from God.

—2 Cor. 1:3-4

The question that God whispered to me rang through my mind again, "What would happen if Christians *didn't* suffer?" I wondered, *Would we be of any value to this hurting world?* I determined the answer was no. We have nothing to offer this hurting world if we've never been hurt and delivered from it.

The Bible says that God "causes his sun to rise on the evil and the good, and sends rain on the righteous and the unrighteous"

(Matt. 5:45). We experience the same sunshine and rain that unbelievers do, the difference is we suffer differently than they do. We are given amazing grace and peace to make it through our hurt. We are carried and are never alone. We suffer with a stubborn joy that comes from our relationship with God. The world looks at us and wonders. Then we can offer the comfort that we ourselves have been given. In our suffering, we are given the gift of a testimony and of being able to truly minister and offer something of value to a world that needs it.

The book, *The Hiding Place* by Corrie ten Boom, illustrates this so beautifully. Corrie and her family were imprisoned in concentration camps during World War II for aiding and hiding Jews from the Nazis. Corrie and her sister, Betsie, suffered greatly in ways that I cannot fathom. While there, Betsie lost her life. In the book, Corrie records Betsie's dream to minister to hurting people: "I leaned down to make out Betsie's words, 'Must tell people what we have learned here. We must tell them that there is no pit so deep that He is not deeper still. They will listen to us, Corrie, because we have been here.'"[1]

Hurting people need people who have been there. They need the hope that only we who have been there can offer. "For just as the sufferings of Christ flow over into our lives, so also through Christ our comfort overflows" (2 Cor. 1:5).

God wants us to bear good fruit, not for ourselves, but so we can give it away to a hungry world. Just as my grandfather trained and pruned his apple orchards to produce the best crops, God sometimes works through the painful circumstances of our lives, like our miscarriages, to bring out our very best. He uses the pain as a form of discipline. This is a discipline that is good and comes from love.

PUNISHMENT VS. DISCIPLINE

In this way, love is made complete among us so that we will have confidence on the day of judgment, because in this world we are like him. There is no fear in love. But perfect love drives out fear, because fear has to do with punishment. The one who fears is not made perfect in love.

—1 John 4:17-18

We live in a world where many embrace philosophies like Karma. "What goes around comes around" is a common belief. That is why we expect punishment when we sin. God does not practice Karma. His way is mercy. He does not give us what we deserve, but instead lavishes grace upon us, giving us what we don't deserve or can't earn.

Punishment is about tearing down, destroying, and hurting someone as payment for what that person has done. Discipline is about training, building up, and making someone stronger so that he or she can be better equipped for what must be faced.

My miscarriages were not punishments, but God did use the opportunity of these trials and even my pain to discipline me. It was the type of discipline that an athlete endures. It came from the heart of a loving Father. I was trained, molded, refined, pruned, made more effective and fruitful, and allowed to better bear my Master's image. Yes, I am a sinner and will continue to sin, but God is making me more like Christ. He promises me, as He does all of us who trust in Him, "He who began a good work in you will carry it on to completion until the day of Christ Jesus" (Phil. 1:6).

GOD DOES LOVE ME

And I pray that you, being rooted and established in love, may have power, together with all the saints, to grasp how wide and long and high and deep is the love of Christ, and to know this love that surpasses knowledge—that you may be filled to the measure of all the fullness of God.

—Eph. 3:17-19

For I am convinced that neither death nor life, neither angels nor demons, neither the present nor the future, nor any powers, neither height nor depth, nor anything else in all creation, will be able to separate us from the love of God that is in Christ Jesus our Lord.

—Rom. 8:38-39

A part of my discipline program was to ask God to shine His light of conviction on my heart and to show me what was in there. I was afraid to do it. I was afraid of what His answer would be, but I prayed David's prayer, "Search me, O God, and know my heart; test me and know my anxious thoughts. Point out anything in me that offends you, and lead me along the path of everlasting life" (Ps. 139:23-24 NLT). I steeled myself for the long "to do" list that would surely follow. I was shocked at God's graciousness in what He revealed. Instead of a long list of offenses, He said, "I want you to really know and believe how much I love you. Don't doubt my love anymore and stop believing the lies that would tell you otherwise."

Romans 8:38-39 says there is nothing that can separate me from His love. Paul's prayer for the Ephesians reveals how important it is for Christians to have a strong and confident grasp of that love. God shouldn't need to prove His love for us. He already did so in the most miraculous way. "But God demonstrates his own love for us in this: While we were still sinners, Christ died for us" (Rom. 5:8).

CONDEMNATION VS. CONVICTION

Therefore, there is now no condemnation for those who are in Christ Jesus.

—Rom. 8:1

If you are a believer in Jesus, and you are feeling condemnation, it is not from God. If past sins are haunting you, seek God for freedom. If you are enslaved to guilt and fear, you will not be effective for the Kingdom.

The Holy Spirit does not condemn, but He does convict. Condemnation and conviction differ in their source and in their purpose. Condemnation comes from the Enemy, but conviction comes from God. Conviction is gentle and leads to repentance. Condemnation sends you running *from* God in shame. Conviction sends you running *to* God for change. We are commanded to live a holy life by God's help, but we are not to live in a state of shame waiting for the axe to fall.

When we have strayed from God's best for our lives and are living contrary to His ways, we open a door for Satan. We open a door for his temptation, accusation, and deceit. These things lead to further sin and estrangement from God. If you have un-confessed sin, confess it quickly. "If we confess our sins, he is faithful and just and will forgive us our sins and purify us from all unrighteousness" (1 John 1:9). Be done with it, stop doing it, and live free from it. After you have agreed with God that it is sin and turned from it in repentance, receive and accept God's forgiveness, and move on. Stop expecting punishment and condemnation from the God who loves you and gave His life to prove it.

Dear Father,

I have believed the Liar who told me You have stopped loving me, and that You are punishing me. Lord, please remove that lie and replace it with your truth. Help me to hear Your voice above all others.

You have proven Your love for me. Forgive me for doubting the completed work Jesus did for me on the cross. He already took my punishment. Thank You for that amazing gift of grace!

Thank You that You are faithful and just to forgive our sins when we confess them. Help me to confess my sins quickly and to accept Your forgiveness and to move on.

Use this time of grief to shape and prune me into the woman You desire me to be. May the result of this time of discipline be a heart that is more beautiful and more useful for Your Kingdom. Give me a testimony and the ability to point this hurting world to You. Thank you for loving me.

In Jesus' Name I pray,
Amen

CHAPTER 5

BUT THIS IS SO UNFAIR!

AVOIDING THE POISON OF BITTERNESS

W HEN ARE YOU going to get angry with God?" my friend
asked me. "I'm waiting for you to shake your fists at Him
and say, 'This isn't fair! I'm mad at you!'"

When I told her I wasn't angry with God, it was the truth, not
because I was a saint, but because my emotions had manifested
in other ways such as fear, anxiety, and depression. Knowing
unresolved anger led to bitterness, I was relieved I wasn't angry. I
didn't want to be a bitter person.

But in reality, I *was* harboring bitterness without recognizing it
for what it was. Thinking bitterness was raging anger held at bay,
I thought I had escaped that particular problem. I wasn't angry
about the situation. Therefore, I wasn't bitter.

Unaware, my bitterness took root inside me subtly. Satan was
sneaky, planting seeds of bitterness through peripheral issues,
instead of the big issue of my babies dying.

Weight gain was one of those peripheral issues. Maintaining
a healthy weight has been a lifelong challenge, and after my girls
were born, I weighed more than I had ever weighed. Determined
to change, I worked hard for two years, losing 36 pounds. Two
girlfriends and I made plans to run a thirteen-mile, half-marathon
race in the spring. In preparation for the race, I was running

between five and eight miles at a time. Four months away from the race, and only eight pounds away from my weight loss goal, I found out I was pregnant with David.

That was the beginning of my miscarriages, and the beginning of a lot of weight gain. Each pregnancy loss added to the number on the scale until I no longer recognized myself. I was consumed with how unfair it all was. Why did I have to work to lose baby weight without a baby to show for it? I was bitter!

The physical side effects of the miscarriages were another peripheral issue. Engorged breasts from milk coming in when you have no baby to feed, is a painful reminder of the injustice. Several embarrassing accidents resulting from incredibly heavy menstrual periods left me humiliated and bitter. It was all so unfair!

With every, "It's so unfair," I uttered, the bitterness took deeper root. The bitterness inside me about the small things was really a reflection of lingering bitterness about the big thing. Not until I seriously searched my heart and specifically looked for it, did I realize the bitterness was even there. Once I identified it, however, a part of me asked, "After all I've been through, don't I deserve a little self pity?"

BUT I'M JUSTIFIED!

"Don't call me Naomi," she responded. "Instead, call me Mara, for the Almighty has made life very bitter for me. I went away full, but the LORD has brought me home empty. Why call me Naomi when the LORD has caused me to suffer and the Almighty has sent such tragedy upon me?"

—Ruth 1:20-21 NLT

In the Bible, the book of Ruth begins with the story of Ruth's mother-in-law, Naomi. Escaping famine, Naomi, her husband Elimelech and their two sons, were forced to leave their home in Bethlehem. After ten years in the foreign country of Moab, Naomi was a widow, destitute, and grieving the deaths of both of her two sons.

Hearing the famine conditions had lifted in Bethlehem, Naomi prepared to return to her home. She was painfully aware of the contrast between how she had left Bethlehem and how she was returning there. She had left full, but now was returning empty, and she was bitter.

I related to Naomi's honesty and sense of entitlement. I never overtly blamed God. I wouldn't think it or even speak it on a conscious level, but deep inside were feelings of bitterness toward Him. Why had He abandoned me? Did He not hear the countless prayers I had prayed for the health and development of my babies? Page after page of my prayer journals were full of my prayers thanking God for my pregnancies and asking Him to protect my babies and to bless their development.

Why? Why did you send me such tragedy, Lord? Feeling like Naomi, I asked, "Aren't I justified in feeling some bitterness?"

The inspiration to get over my feelings of needing to be justified and to begin the hard work of getting rid of the bitterness, came from three sources: two memories from my childhood, a popular song on the radio, and a warning from the Bible.

HOWARD AND THE LADY WHO WAVED

Howard was my next-door neighbor when I was a little girl. He was mean and bitter! Rarely leaving his house, he would yell at kids through his window. One morning I took the brunt of his anger for jumping rope on my front porch too early in the morning. That morning he actually left his house, so he could stand on his porch to yell obscenities at me and shake his fist. He was a bitter old man who was determined to make the rest of the world as miserable as he was. He became a model of the type of old person I did not want to become.

"The Lady Who Waved" was a celebrity in Oak Harbor, Washington, when I was a teenager. She was an elderly lady who walked everyday and did not let a single car pass her without a wave and a smile. The local newspaper ran an exposé on her, highlighting her impact on the people of our town. It was impossible to drive by her without feeling good. She had a permanent smile on her face and brightened the day of anyone who had the good fortune of driving past her. I remember thinking, *I want to be like her when I'm old.*

Two people at the end of their lives: One miserable and bitter, bent on sucking anyone into his misery. The other was radiant and joyful, spreading that joy to anyone who crossed her path. Who do I want to become? I want to be "The Lady Who Waves."

Everyone will suffer in this life. There is no escaping that fact. We may look at others who are in a season of blessing and think, *They don't have to suffer like me.* Suffering, sickness, grief, and pain will touch everyone's life. Why do some arrive at the end of their lifetime like Howard, twisted with disdain, misery, and bitterness, while others arrive at the end like "The Lady Who Waves"? The answer is how we choose to respond each and every time we face heartache.

We must choose either to reach out to God for healing or turn toward ourselves like wounded birds refusing to allow the Healer near us. We either dwell on injustices and wallow in how unfair life is, or honestly present our feelings to the Lord, asking Him to remove the bitterness. Wounded hearts will become calloused and scarred if pain and bitterness are ignored. If we do not allow God to dig out the root of bitterness, it will remain, poisoning us and defiling others. Unchecked, we all become like Howard. Held in the arms of the Healer, we become the Lady Who Waved.

Christa Wells' song "Held," performed by Natalie Grant, became my anthem. The line, "To think that Providence would take a child from his mother while she prays is appalling"[1] captured my feelings exactly, but the words of the song modeled the wisdom of avoiding bitterness instead of giving into it. I began to focus on the biblical truth that believers in Christ were not promised an escape *from* heartache. Rather they will be loved, held, and empowered to live *through* the heartache.

The lyrics of the song portrayed the real emotions I was feeling, and then pointed to a better way than bitterness. I wanted to *taste* the bitterness and let the hatred *numb* my sorrow, but this response would have proven debilitating. The world and the Enemy tell us we have the right to be bitter after loss, assuring us we deserve it. Embracing this lie leads to our destruction and not to our peace.

The Bible warns that giving into it also has the ability to harm more than just ourselves.

BITTERNESS DEFILES OTHERS

See to it that no one misses the grace of God and that no bitter root grows up to cause trouble and defile many.

—Heb. 12:15

The Bible warns us to get rid of the bitter root before it grows up, causes trouble, and defiles many. Those recognizing bitterness in themselves must seriously fight it. We are not the only ones affected by lingering bitterness in our hearts. Bitter people suck others into their misery. Dictionary.com defines the word *defile* as "To make filthy or dirty, pollute."[2]

The poison of bitterness pollutes our cherished homes and relationships. We cannot allow ourselves to become someone who defiles many because of our choices in response to suffering. Failing to go to the Lord with our bitterness, puts our children, our spouses, our friends, and our family at risk. We will become hard and the seeping poison of bitterness will defile those we love the most.

WHAT'S IN MY HEART GOD?

Search me, O God, and know my heart; test me and know my anxious thoughts. See if there is any offensive way in me, and lead me in the way everlasting.

—Ps. 139:23-24

Fighting bitterness begins with allowing God to reveal the true condition of our hearts. Personally, I didn't even know I was harboring unhealthy bitterness, but God wasn't ignorant to that fact. The Scripture above is from a psalm King David wrote about how God knows us intimately. There is no place we can go from His presence. He knows our thoughts and words before we even speak them. He knows our hearts better than we know them ourselves.

God, our Great Physician, desires to heal our wounds. When we ask Him to reveal the condition of our hearts, He will pinpoint the areas that are making us spiritually sick. We won't be able to cooperate with God's fight against our bitterness if we don't know it's there. If we want to avoid the poison of bitterness, we first need to ask God to reveal it to us.

NAMING THE DRAGON

The thief comes only to steal and kill and destroy; I have come that they may have life, and have it to the full.
—John 10:10

My dad taught me "in order to slay the dragon you have to name it." The fight against bitterness also requires identifying the true Enemy in our suffering. When Satan whispers in your ear, "How could a loving God take your baby from you? How can you trust God for anything now? He obviously doesn't care about you. Look what He's done to you!" he deflects our attention away from himself, our true Enemy, and onto God, where the blame does not belong.

Jesus called Satan a thief and said he comes only to steal, kill, and destroy. Sin has corrupted what God has desired for us and brought sorrow. The author of sin is Satan. He is the dragon. Satan and the sin inside us are our Enemies. Christ offers hope! He is not the one we should be bitter toward. When Satan lies about our precious God, point your finger right back at him! After naming the dragon, it is possible to move on to the next step in the battle: recognizing God's right to do what He will.

GOD IS GOD AND I AM NOT

Where were you when I laid the earth's foundation? Tell me, if you understand. Who marked off its dimensions? Surely you know! Who stretched a measuring line across it? On what were its footings set, or who laid its cornerstone- while the morning stars sang together and all the angels shouted for joy? Who shut up the sea behind doors when it burst forth from the womb, when I made the clouds its garment and wrapped it in thick darkness, when I fixed limits for it and set its doors and bars in place, when I said, "This far you may come and no farther; here is where your proud waves halt?"

—Job 38:4-11

Slaying pride is another step in the fight against bitterness. Following the tragedy of September 11, 2001, Steven Curtis Chapman released a song called, "God is God." I sing it often when I am struggling. The lyrics remind us that life is uncertain. We often have questions without answers, leaving only one conclusion, "God is God and I am not."[3] The final line of the song exhorts us to worship God because He alone is worthy of that worship.

Circumstances often leave us with more questions than answers. One answer I do have is, God is God and I am not. So much of our bitterness comes from pride. Our hearts scream, "Why did You do it this way, Lord. There had to be a better way. I could have done it better!" Job 38 reminds us we couldn't do it better. We weren't there when God laid the foundations of the earth. We have no clue how He confines the oceans to their specific locations. Since we cannot begin to fathom how creation works, how can we arrogantly scold the Creator for conducting our lives His way? The only healthy response is to submit to Him and to worship Him, regardless of our unanswered questions.

CALL IT WHAT IT IS

If we confess our sins, he is faithful and just and will forgive us our sins and purify us from all unrighteousness.

—1 John 1:9

The final and most important step in fighting bitterness is repentance. I had to call it what it was. Sin. I had to confess it to God who already knew but was faithful to forgive. When we identify sin as sin, and stop making excuses for it in our lives, we shine light on it and it loses its power over us.

It is difficult to tell a grieving mother who has just lost a precious and longed for baby, that she is sinning when she feels bitterness.

How can we help it when bitter thoughts pop into our head? How can we be held accountable for an emotion? The problem is, we so often think of sin as things we do, forgetting that sin is a part of our nature. We have inherited a sin nature, so when we recognize sin in us, instead of condemnation, we can just call it what it is and not be a slave to it any longer. The Word says He is faithful and just and will forgive us our sins, and purify us. I need His purification often. I do not want the consequences of bitterness in my life, and God doesn't want that for me either.

The root of bitterness cannot be uprooted by our own strength. Rejoicing in painful circumstances is contrary to our very nature. We can pretend to be happy, on the outside, but if bitterness remains, it is a counterfeit joy. You cannot fake joy. Bitterness must be uprooted by God for us. When we submit to Him and ask Him to do it for us on a day-by-day, moment-by-moment basis, then we will be free and will avoid the poison of bitterness that can ruin us and ruin those around us.

Dear Father,

The Bible warns that bitterness is a poison that can cause trouble in our lives and defile people around us. The Enemy, the world, and my "self" tell me the opposite, that I am justified to feel bitter. Please help me to be free from the poison of bitterness as I heal from the heartache of my miscarriage.

Search my heart and show me what is in it that You want to heal. I confess the bitterness that is there and call it what it is: sin. Forgive me and purify me as Your Word promises You will do. Thank you that You do not condemn me for the sin that is there, but long to free me and to protect me from the consequences of a bitter heart. Help me to rejoice in You and to trust in You.

In Jesus' Name I pray,
Amen

CHAPTER 6

SATAN THE ULTIMATE BULLY

SURVIVING SPIRITUAL ATTACK

Be self-controlled and alert. Your enemy the devil prowls around like a roaring lion looking for someone to devour.

—1 Pet. 5:8

ONE OF THE furthest things from my mind after my miscarriages was spiritual warfare. It didn't occur to me to think about it. Certainly none of the miscarriage literature I was given mentioned it, nor did any of the sympathy cards I received. Can you imagine a card saying, "By the way, just wanted to warn you Satan and his demons will be after you. Get ready!"

As I look back, I can see so much evidence of spiritual bombardment. It would have been nice to have been forewarned it was coming, so I could have been better prepared. Actually, as a Christian I *was* warned. I just forgot.

The Bible warns that our Enemy prowls around like a roaring lion looking for someone to devour. It reminds me of the nature films I've watched where a lion is stalking a herd of antelopes or gazelles. He seeks out the weakest members of the herd, usually the babies or the injured. My miscarriages had left me spiritually weak and injured. I was an easy target for the flaming arrows of fear, doubt, guilt, discouragement, bitterness, and lies.

I would think at times like this I should be able to call a time out, "I'm injured here; could you kindly give me a break until I'm well enough to fight back?" Unfortunately, there are no time-outs or breaks from this battle. Satan doesn't work this way. He is the ultimate bully. When you are down, he doesn't sit back and wait for a fair fight. He rushes in and starts kicking you before you have a chance to stand and fight back.

A SUBTLE ATTACK

I am fully convinced I encountered strong spiritual attack following the losses of my babies, but it wasn't as if I heard voices or saw satanic symbols drawn in the fog on my mirror when I stepped out of the shower. The pictures on my walls weren't spinning. Nothing was levitating in my house. Instead of dramatic, spooky things that would have been obviously evil, the Enemy used subtlety and snuck in unnoticed.

Fear was one of the biggest issues I struggled with after my miscarriages. I would fear for my daughters' safety. I would think thoughts like, *Maybe, I'm not a good enough parent, so God is going to take away each of my children from me one by one.*

In addition, I'd fear for my husband's safety at work as a police officer. When he was on duty, I'd think things like, *Maybe Pat is next.* It was almost as if I expected officers to knock on my door some night and tell me something had happened to him. My imagination ran wild with the fear: which of my loved ones God was going to take from me next?

What about my own safety? Obviously, God wasn't concerned about me anymore. He hadn't protected me from this pain, so how could I ever feel safe again? The doors of my imagination were thrown wide open to the morbid possibilities of what could happen to me now: rape, abduction, murder, car accident, being buried alive . . . anything was possible, right? I felt vulnerable and afraid.

Fear was joined by self-doubt. Intellectually, I understood God's grace and I was just as valuable as anyone else, but in my heart I'd hear and believe messages such as, *You aren't really saved. You are going to stand before God someday and He is going to tell you "You have failed and are going to hell." He doesn't really love you. He's angry with you, punishing you, and you're going to have to earn His favor back.* Other messages entered my mind like, *You're ugly, fat, and worthless. You better just stay home, so no one sees how far you've let yourself go.*

I would only go out in public if I was completely put together with a shower, make-up, and had on the right clothes. Even after all of my preparation to leave the house, I hated who I was and what I looked like. If I realized I was about to run into someone at church or out shopping whom I hadn't seen in a while, I'd turn and walk the other way, so they couldn't see me and judge me.

There was also a barrage of temptation. Ashamed as I was about my weight gain, I found myself unable to resist using food for comfort. It was the easiest way I could find to self-medicate. Every day I'd try to get it under control. I'd wake-up thinking, *okay, today I'm going to diet*, only to find myself giving into temptation. I felt so discouraged about my failure, I'd run to the pantry for more, thinking, *I am such a failure! Why bother trying?*

I also experienced strange, random thoughts that didn't feel as if I had thought them, but more like they had been planted in my mind. Sometimes they were sinful. Sometimes they were scary. I'd just try to shake them off and think, *Ooh, that was a bad thought.* I was still unaware of being involved in spiritual conflict, however. I was deceived into believing all of this was true and the new reality of who I had become.

AFRAID TO FIGHT BACK

Eventually, God worked on my heart. Through Bible study and prayer times, He began revealing to me the many ways I was experiencing spiritual attack. He also showed me how I was bound to things I didn't have to be. It took more than two years for me to fully realize what was going on. When I finally identified the source of the problems, I wasn't sure I wanted to do anything about it.

Growing up as a Christian, I had been taught that spiritual warfare existed. I knew the Bible taught believers to be on guard against the devil. My problem was that I was afraid of the devil. The whole idea of being involved in fighting demons or Satan was way beyond my comfort zone.

Satan had convinced me he was too powerful and scary for me to even think about. I believed it was better to ignore the spiritual realm because I wasn't powerful enough to take him on. Fighting back seemed like an invitation for more spiritual attack. I continued to take the beating because I was too afraid to consider fighting back. I wanted to pretend Satan and demons didn't exist because facing their reality was just too scary.

Identifying Our Struggle

For our struggle is not against flesh and blood, but against the rulers, against the authorities, against the powers of this dark world and against the spiritual forces of evil in the Heavenly realms.

—Eph. 6:12

Awareness that we aren't exempt from spiritual warfare when we are grieving is an important first step to surviving this attack. When we become Christians, we are immediately a part of the battle. In his book, *The Fight*, John White puts it this way, "To acknowledge Jesus as Savior and Lord is to join an army. Whether you know it or not, you have enlisted."[1] Closing your eyes and pretending it doesn't exist won't stop the battle.

Thankfully, this battle is not dependent upon our own strength or power. God promises the Enemy will be defeated "not by might nor by power, but by my Spirit" (Zech. 4:6-7). Yes, we can expect Satan to come in like a flood, while we are grieving the losses of our babies. However, in our weakness we can still be victorious by God's Spirit and by His power and not by our own.

When I began to recognize the signs of spiritual attack, God in his graciousness, provided strategies to oppose the Enemy. He gave me tools to fight back even in my weakness.

Worship: A Powerful Weapon

About midnight Paul and Silas were praying and singing hymns to God, and the other prisoners were listening to them. Suddenly there was such a violent earthquake that the foundations of the prison were shaken. At once all the prison doors flew open, and everybody's chains came loose.

—Acts 16:25-26

The first tool that I needed was to develop a life of worship. At the time, I didn't realize that by listening to Christian music, I was using an effective spiritual weapon. I knew I was spiritually weak, and during times of depression, it was difficult for me to read or focus on preaching, so I relied a lot on music. I listened because I couldn't do anything else. I left the radio playing all day long on a Christian radio station. Soon, messages of hope and messages of God's greatness and love were filling my heart and mind. Truth pushed out the lies I was hearing from the Enemy. I began to join in the singing. I put aside my circumstances and pain, and sang praise to my God who is great despite my circumstances. My miscarriages didn't mean that His character had changed or that His worthiness had diminished. Satan wanted me to believe they had, but the truth was that God was worthy of worship despite my pain. He is worthy. Period.

Music and singing are not the only way to worship. Worship is a heart condition. Music, reading God's Word, and speaking truth about Him, are all wonderful conduits of praise and worship. I love to read out loud the praises David wrote in the Psalms. When I can't think of words myself, I often rely on words of praise that others have written in the Bible and make them my own. Worshipping God in whatever form, from the heart and with sincerity, is an important weapon in spiritual warfare.

Satan often attacks our dependence on God. Worship reaffirms our dependence on Him. Satan tempts us away from God with distractions, counterfeit spirituality, food, drugs, sex . . . you fill in the blank. Worship reminds us of how worthy God is of our dependence.

Paul and Silas modeled worship in difficult circumstances for us. In Acts 16 we read that they were falsely accused, beaten severely, and thrown into the deepest part of prison. In our modern, clean world, it is difficult to imagine the conditions of their prison. The darkness and smell of the innermost part of the prison—the place where the most vile offenders were kept—or the physical, mental, and emotional pain that Paul and Silas endured, must have been horrific. They didn't know how long they were to be there, and the injustices of their imprisonment could have tortured them. Instead of bitterness or anger at God, the result of their worship was freedom, victory, and deliverance. We can experience that same kind of deliverance through worship.

THE FATHER OF LIES

He was a murderer from the beginning, not holding to the truth, for there is no truth in him. When he lies, he speaks his native language, for he is a liar and the father of lies.

—John 8:44

The next tool God gave me was the tool of truth. I was afraid to think about Satan and demonic influences or attacks because I was listening to Satan's native language: lies. His greatest weapon is to lie to us and to convince us we are too helpless and powerless to fight him. He wants us to believe he is God's equal. He tells us he is the opposite of God, making us forget in actuality, he is a created being and the already defeated Enemy of God. He is nowhere near God's equal. He is not omnipresent, he cannot read my mind, and he can't compel me to do anything.

The incompetence I felt in dealing with spiritual attack is a common misconception among believers. Many of us have believed the lie that we need some special spiritual power in order to face-off with the devil. We don't need power, what we need is *truth*. In the book, *The Bondage Breaker*, Neil T. Anderson says, "I have learned from the Scriptures and my personal experience that *truth* is the liberating agent. The power of Satan is in the lie, and the power of the believer is in knowing the truth. We are to pursue *truth*, not power."[2]

The truth is Satan is already defeated. The only power he has over me is the power I allow him to have. James 4:7 tells us, "So humble yourselves before God. Resist the devil, and he will flee from you" (NLT). The key is to resist him by knowing the truth, speaking the truth, and believing the truth, not by a power encounter.

He will not flee because he is afraid of me, or because of any power or authority I may possess. On the contrary, I know I am nothing apart from Christ! Christ has already defeated the devil for me. I am free in Him. In Him, I can cling to the truths of God's Word and stop believing the lies of the devil. If I resist, he must flee because he is no match for our Lord.

We find the truth we need in the Bible. Attending Bible study consistently aids my healing. I need to keep learning and soaking up truth. I need the Bible to become more and more familiar to me so I can know where to find what I need.

As a Bible study leader, I see women who are intimidated by the Bible. They are insecure about their lack of knowledge concerning where to find Scriptures. They watch the veterans flipping from this place to that place, saying things like, "That reminds me of verse so and so." The less experienced Bible student's eyes bug out, and I can just about read their minds as they think, *How do they do that? Have they memorized the entire Bible or something?*

I reassure my ladies that familiarity with the Bible comes with exposure. It is similar to when you first move to a new city. At first, you have difficulty even remembering how to get to the grocery store and it is so easy to get lost. A year later, however, you can go anywhere you need to go. It is the same with the Bible. The more time you spend in it, the more you become familiar with where things are. It is so important to be familiar with the Bible because knowing the truth is critical to combating Satan's lies.

THE BATTLEFIELD

For though we live in the world, we do not wage war as the world does. The weapons we fight with are not the weapons of the world. On the contrary, they have divine power to demolish strongholds. We demolish arguments and every pretension that sets itself up against the knowledge of God, and we take captive every thought to make it obedient to Christ.

—2 Cor. 10:3-5

Don't copy the behavior and customs of this world, but let God transform you into a new person by changing the way you think. Then you will learn to know God's will for you, which is good and pleasing and perfect.

—Rom. 12:2 NLT

We fight this spiritual war upon the battlefield of our minds. It takes self-discipline to work at changing our thinking to align it with God's truth and will for our lives.

During my counseling sessions, my counselor asked me to read the book *Search for Significance* by Robert S. McGee. I cannot recommend it highly enough. It was life changing. I must agree with Billy Graham when he says, "*The Search for Significance* should be read by every Christian."

In the final chapter of the book, McGee teaches a process for *how* to take captive every thought to make it obedient to Christ. The process he suggests can be summarized as identify-repent-reject-replace.[3] This formula became my greatest defense in the battle for my mind.

Here is an example of how I have used it in my life. If I recognize a lie that I have believed as truth, such as "You should be afraid," I would first identify it as a lie. Next, I would repent of believing that lie. "Father, I have believed the lie that I should be living in fear. Forgive me for allowing myself to be captive to fear and the lies of the Enemy."

The next step is to reject the lie. "I will no longer believe I should live in fear. I will not be captive to such a lie any more." Finally, the lie is replaced with truth from God's Word. "The Bible exhorts us to fear not, and Romans 8:15 says, 'For you did not receive a spirit that makes you a slave again to fear, but you received the spirit of sonship. And by Him we cry, "Abba, Father."'"

Actively stopping Satan's lies as they enter my mind, taking them captive, and replacing them with truth is liberating. Truth really does set us free.

Not every thought entering our mind comes from Satan. Some things we think up all by ourselves. It was critical for me to pray over my thoughts. I needed to ask God to guide my thoughts and to reveal self-deception. Paul's reminder to the Romans, "Don't copy the behavior and customs of this world, but let God transform you into a new person by changing the way you think. Then you will learn to know God's will for you, which is good and pleasing and perfect" (Rom. 12:2 NLT), was and is an important tool in winning the battle for my mind. To be free from the falsehoods that were stealing my joy, I needed to ask God to change the way I thought.

PRAYING FOR JOY

The joy of the LORD is your strength.
—Neh. 8:10

Bring joy to your servant, for to you, O Lord, I lift up my soul.
—Ps. 86:4

If the joy of the Lord is our strength, then it makes sense that discouragement is an ofen-used tool of the Enemy. We are stripped of our strength when we are stripped of joy. Another tool God gave me to defeat the work of the enemy was to ask for renewed joy. God wants us to run to him whenever we are discouraged and to ask along with the Psalmist, "Bring joy to your servant, for to you, O Lord, I lift up my soul" (Ps. 86:4).

Satan wants us to be defeated and ineffective for God's Kingdom. When we are discouraged, defeated, and depressed, we will not make an impact on this world. We will not lead souls to the Lord.

God is the giver of real and lasting joy. We don't need false or counterfeit joy or a fake happiness. We need the joy that only God can give when we ask Him for it.

IT's A LIFESTYLE

God has graciously equipped me to fight against the enemy who wished to destroy me in my weakness and grief. He wants the same victory for you. We do not need to remain in bondage to Satan and his attacks. We have already been set free. When we worship God regardless of our circumstances, when we exchange lies for truth, when we pray for right thinking and joy, and when we strive to live a righteous life by Christ's power, we will survive and experience victory over spiritual attack.

Fascination with demonic activity takes our eyes off Jesus and the glory of God. As Anderson exhorts us, "We are not to be demon-centered; we are to be God-centered and ministry-centered. We are to fix our eyes on Jesus, preach the gospel, love one another, and be God's ambassadors in our fallen world."

This has been a challenging chapter to write. I continue to war against many of these issues. I am not perfect, I still give into temptation, I still forget to resist the enemy, and I still believe and act on things that are not true. I am imperfect, but I am growing. The important goal for me has not been perfection, but persistence in fighting the good fight.

Dean Sherman in his book, *Spiritual Warfare for Every Christian*, reminds believers that, "Spiritual warfare is not just a prayer prayed or a demon rebuked—it is a life lived."[4] I'm a Christian, so I am a warrior. I join Paul in declaring, "I press on toward the goal to win the prize for which God has called me Heavenward in Christ Jesus" (Phil. 3:14).

Be victorious in Christ. Refuse to live a life of bondage. Choose the freedom you have already been given. Don't give up!

Dear Father,

    My grief has made me an easy target for spiritual attack. I didn't expect spiritual warfare to be a part of this grieving process. Please equip me with all I need to be on guard against the Enemy.

    Satan would have me believe he is too powerful and scary to even think about, but I cling to the promise that the One who is within me is "greater than the one that is in the world" (1 John 4:4). I am so thankful this battle is not dependent upon my strength or power, but on Your Holy Spirit.

    Truth is a powerful weapon. Help me to believe what is true about You and my circumstances. Help me to know the Bible and to apply it to my life. Show me how to replace lies with the truth of Your Word.

    Please restore joy where it is lacking and remove all fear. I refuse to live a life of bondage. I choose the freedom that is mine in Christ. Thank you for the victory You have already accomplished on my behalf. I worship You!

In Jesus' Name I pray,
Amen

CHAPTER 7

DID SHE REALLY JUST

SAY THAT?

RECEIVING COMMENTS WITH GRACE

Hatred stirs up dissension, but love covers over all wrongs.
—Prov. 10:12

"M AYBE YOUR BABIES would have been retarded."
"Maybe Mother Nature is trying to tell you something."
"You should be happy that your children are in Heaven, because they may have rejected Christ and gone to hell."
"How many kids do you want anyway?"
"Sticks and stones may break my bones, but words will never hurt me." *Whatever!* What a lie! Words leave deeper wounds than sticks and stones, and when you are grieving, inevitably, people will say the wrong things and you will be hurt.

As I dwelt on their words, anger boiled to the surface because of their insensitivity. Yet, I often wondered if God was sending me a message through them. Confusion added to the hurt.

After my first pregnancy loss, I decided I needed a strategy for dealing with insensitive words. Everytime someone offered me condolences or advice, I would remember to look at the heart of the person and the motivation behind what they were saying instead of judging their choice of words. The truth is, most people were afraid they were going to say the wrong thing. Feeling helpless about

AND THEN YOU WERE GONE

how they should offer it, yet longing to be a comfort, this fear led some people to avoid saying anything at all. Others pulled away when I needed them more than ever. I learned to be thankful that friends and family were trying and they weren't avoiding the subject or pretending it had never happened. I became grateful for their expression of love, valuing that more than the words themselves.

This change of heart was a gift from God as He taught me to receive words with grace. Satan often uses words to stir up dissension. He plants bitterness and an inability to forgive, which separate us from the relationships we cherish. I learned to value the precious relationships in my life, rather than allowing Satan to destroy them over something as petty as a few wrong words spoken out of love.

Reassuring my friends and family they *couldn't* say the wrong thing, I freed them from a lot of stress. Deciding to filter all words through love, I enabled them to comfort me. I began to receive comfort and wisdom from words that previously I would have regarded as insensitive.

RESENTING THE TRUTH

Apply your heart to instruction and your ears to words of knowledge.
—Prov. 23:12

Gold there is, and rubies in abundance, but lips that speak knowledge are a rare jewel.
—Prov. 20:15

Sometimes the words we initially receive as insensitive are truth. While I was still grieving, a lady in Bible study exhorted me to be excited about the return of Christ. "Just think! Jesus could return at any moment and you will be reunited with your babies." Joy was shining from her eyes, and I knew she was really looking forward to that event and wanted it to be a comfort to me. Instead of receiving these words with grace, I resented them. I felt she was saying I was wrong to be grieving.

60

The reality is the words she spoke to me were true. The Bible calls us to be encouraged as we look for the return of Christ. God has provided us with this hope to help us during grief. I knew this with my head, but my heart responded with resentment. As I examined my heart following that conversation, I discovered two things:

1. Pride: I didn't want to be *told* this; I already knew it.

2. Rebellion: I didn't *want* to be encouraged by these words; I wanted my babies, not the rapture.

It was at this moment I realized most of the words I had considered insensitive had the capacity to carry truth I didn't want to face. My prideful heart was distorting the truth. The things people said that hurt weren't always the best choice to offer me at the time, but in many cases, there were some nuggets of truth. It is *true* that my babies could have had physical or mental problems that could have led to great suffering in this life. It is *true* that my babies are already in Heaven without having to make a decision or having faced the temptation to reject Christ. It is *true* that Heaven is more wonderful than I can imagine. It is *true* that I should be content with the blessings I have already received. It is also *true* that all things happen for a reason.

Identifying pride and resentment was critical to healing as I accepted words from wise friends. I could have missed being encouraged by the truth of these words if I hadn't learned to recognize the deception in my own heart that was rejecting truth.

WHAT ARE YOU TRYING TO SAY GOD?

It is important to examine your heart for pride, rebellion, or deception that distorts the truth, but that does not mean all words spoken by people are to be received as divine direction for your life. My vulnerability caused me to hear all words as if they were God-spoken messages.

As I was being wheeled into surgery following my third miscarriage, I shared with the nurse and the anesthesiologist a little about my history. The last words I remember hearing as I went under were those of the anesthesiologist saying, "Maybe Mother Nature is trying to tell you something." Following the procedure, the recovery nurse asked about our family and my miscarriages and ended the conversation with, "Well, how many kids do you want anyway?"

Although these comments came from a secular, worldly perspective, their words still floated around in my head. I don't believe in Mother Nature, but was God trying to tell me something? Was I a bad mother and He didn't trust me with more children? Was He trying to teach my family and me contentment with what He had already given us? If we kept trying, would He take the life of all future babies, too? What message was I supposed to be getting? I kept asking, "What are you trying to say, God?"

Eventually, I had to give it up. Although each person offering advice sincerely desired to be helpful, their words weren't necessarily prophetic, nor was I meant to take each sentence as "Thus sayeth the Lord!" I needed the discernment that can only come from the Holy Spirit. Only He could show us which words were applicable to our lives and which were not.

Maybe You Were Just Meant to Adopt

A primary issue requiring the discernment of the Holy Spirit was the comments I received regarding adoption.

"Have you ever thought that maybe you were just meant to adopt?" These words usually came from some nice woman who had never adopted a child and had given birth to her own slew of healthy children. Every woman who has miscarried or struggled with infertility has faced this question. Intending to offer hope, the motivation behind the question is, "Perhaps God has a different plan to make you a mother, bringing joy to you and to a child somewhere who doesn't have a mother. Wouldn't this be a beautiful thing?" Instead, I heard "You aren't good enough to give birth to your own child like I can." I've even known women who went so far as to think people were actually saying, "God killed your baby so you would be willing to adopt." Whatever the grieving woman hears, her emotion is often anger. Again, it is critical to judge the heart and not the words alone.

There are several reasons why this particular question is difficult to accept when we are grieving. We can feel as if we are being offered a consolation prize and resent it. We can feel anger at God and think, *Maybe God did take my baby so I'd be willing to adopt.* We can be afraid that God is going to force this on us, whether we like it or not.

My initial reaction to this question was fear. I feared that if I even considered adoption, I wouldn't be allowed to have another biological child as I wanted. I would have to kill that dream inside of me. I was afraid that when I opened myself up to the needs of motherless children, I would be compelled to choose adoption as a matter of conscience or duty.

As I struggled with this, I watched good friends of mine go through the adoption process after years of painful infertility. Watching them took all that fear away. I was struck with the joy on their faces as they prepared for their adoption. They anticipated it with the same joy I had anticipated the births of my daughters. They weren't struggling to resign themselves to a less desirable option. They desired this adoption with a passion God had placed in their hearts. He had given them a new dream and it was from Him. It was His work in them, not something they had to resign themselves to or struggle to accept. It was a beautiful thing. It was something I did not need to fear.

I was able to relax and not resent someone asking me the question anymore. If God wanted us to adopt, He would do the work in us of planting and growing that dream, and it would not be second best. He would replace one dream with another equally wonderful dream. And until He did that in my heart and Pat's heart, I could accept the question. People just wanted to give me another option to think about because they loved me and wanted me to be happy.

God does not take our babies and then offer adoption as a consolation prize. He doesn't see some woman as "meant to adopt" and then strike her with miscarriage or infertility. We are not all called to adopt, even if we have suffered a miscarriage or struggled through years of infertility. If we are truly trusting God, we can relax and not worry that He is going to make us adopt when we don't want to.

On the other hand, God often does use adoption to bring beauty out of suffering. We live in a fallen world and God always works what was intended for evil into something beautiful (see Romans 8:28). Couples suffer as they grieve a miscarriage or an inability to conceive. They long to have a child. Orphans also suffer as they long for a home and loving parents. God sees the suffering and He acts, creating the desire for adoption in the hearts of couples.

When God spoke to Moses in the burning bush, He said, "I have indeed seen the misery of my people in Egypt. I have heard them crying out because of their slave drivers, and I am concerned about their suffering" (Ex. 3:7). He saw the suffering of the Israelites at the hands of the Egyptians and He acted. I see this same heart when He brings joy to a suffering family and a family to a suffering orphan through adoption. God is the God of the individual, and He can see what will be best for us.

If we close our minds and harden our hearts to the thought of adoption, we are telling God we do not trust Him with our future. Jorie Kincaid in her book *Adopting for Good,* put it this way as she portrayed the bigger picture that God sees: "Those circumstances that seem to be second-best may not be second-best at all!"[1]

When I opened myself up to the possibility of adopting, I really enjoyed the research I began to do. I read an entire book in one sitting. I couldn't get enough. Reading testimonies of how God has worked through adoption has encouraged me so much. I learned how He is the God of the individual and hears the cries of the orphans and sees the broken hearts of families who long for children. Even if we never adopt, I am grateful to be made aware of the needs of orphans worldwide, so I can pray and offer support in whatever way I can.

I can now appreciate the words of someone who asks us if we have considered adoption because we should consider it without fear, resentment, or rebellion. Proverbs 16:9 reminds us that, "In his heart a man plans his course, but the LORD determines his steps." He has a plan for each of us. The important thing is that we do not allow a hard heart to keep us from being led in whatever direction He is calling us.

THE EARNEST COUNSEL OF GOOD FRIENDS

Perfume and incense bring joy to the heart, and the pleasantness of one's friend springs from his earnest counsel.

—Prov. 27:9

Receiving comments regarding the adoption question as well as all comments offered during grief requires the covering of grace and a heart willing to listen to the discernment of the Holy Spirit. The important thing is to value and cherish your relationships enough to protect them. When we lost each baby, I leaned hard on my friends. It was so good to talk things out and have people who were willing to listen. It was also good to receive their healing words. I could have lost that without a covering of grace and discernment.

Choosing to receive insensitive comments with grace takes discipline. It is not easy, but your precious relationships are worth the effort. To have people who love you is such a blessing and it is one worth protecting.

Dear Father,

I pray that during this time of grieving, You would equip me with the ability to accept all words with grace. Help me to see the heart and motivation of the words being spoken far above the actual words themselves. Give me a heart of gratitude for the love being expressed by the words of condolence and advice. Help me to remember how much people fear saying the wrong thing, and show me how to free them from that fear. I am so thankful for their support and I do not want to push them away.

Please prevent Satan from stirring up dissension in my heart or from making me overly sensitive. Do not allow him to destroy these relationships that are so precious to me.

Search my heart and help me to see where pride, rebellion, or deception may be making me overly sensitive, or causing me to reject truth. Provide me with the discernment of the Holy Spirit You have promised. Make my heart soft and able to hear truth when it is spoken.

Grant me wisdom to know what You are teaching my heart, and the discernment to let go of the words that are not of You. Heal the hurt coming from reckless words, and grant me the ability to forgive those who speak them.

Thank you for the grace You have shown me. Give me Your heart of love.

In Jesus' Name I pray,
Amen

CHAPTER 8

CLIMBING OUT OF THE PIT OF

DESPAIR

CONQUERING DEPRESSION

He lifted me out of the slimy pit, out of the mud and mire; he set
my feet on a rock and gave me a firm place to stand.

—Ps. 40:2

M Y FRIENDS AND family weren't shocked when I became
depressed. Obviously, my body and emotions had taken a toll.
What seemed to surprise them was the suddenness with which it
came. My friend said, "It's so strange how one day you were fine,
and then overnight you seemed to crash."

To the outside observer it probably did appear sudden, but I
felt it coming long before it got the better of me. I valiantly fought
the storm clouds as they rolled in, threatening to consume me. I
knew I was sinking, yet I didn't have the strength to fight. Then
one day, I woke up in the pit.

I sleepwalked through my days. The pain showed on my face. I
felt old and unattractive. I craved sleep, yet when bedtime arrived,
a nervous, restless energy kept me up late. Hours disappeared as I
sat in front of the computer mindlessly playing solitaire or Yahtzee,
finding anything to avoid lying in bed facing the darkness and
pain.

I longed to be a hermit. Being around other people was such hard work! One Saturday, so overwhelmed by the mere thought of going to the Saturday night service at our church, I wrote this in my prayer journal:

I'm so empty. I have nothing to offer other people. It makes my head hurt just to follow conversations. I'm dreading church tonight even though I know it is the best place for me to be. Please help me. Don't let me come up with excuses that prevent me from being there. Dreading it coming is not good, and it is leaving me unable to get going this morning. Help me to just take this day one step at a time instead of being so overwhelmed.

I hurt people I cared about as I retreated from offers of friendship. Life overwhelmed me, and I didn't have it in me to maintain relationships.

There was a distinct point when I could no longer deny my need for help. Making the decision to call my family doctor was the easy part. Actually doing it was another story. I sat at the kitchen counter staring at the telephone for two hours. Here I was, a fairly intelligent, grown woman, unable to make a simple doctor appointment. My husband found me and took over. He arranged the doctor appointment, stayed home from work, and made sure I got to the clinic. Later that day, I sat in front of my doctor too emotional even to speak. "Well, I can see you are obviously in a lot of pain," He said. He prescribed medication and added, "I also think you need to get some grief counseling."

Counseling? I don't know why, but it wasn't difficult for me to admit I needed an antidepressant. My body had been through a lot, so I assumed my hormones were out of whack. I just wanted whatever pill would make me normal again. However, counseling, was a different matter! That insinuated I was weak in the head. Ashamed, I came home and admitted to Pat that the doctor thought I needed counseling. We scheduled an appointment with a Christian counselor for the following day. That phone call was an important first step in my climb out of the pit.

WE ARE ALL A PART OF THE BODY

But in fact God has arranged the parts in the body, every one of them, just as he wanted them to be. If they were all one part, where would the body be? As it is, there are many parts, but one body. The eye cannot say to the hand, "I don't need you!" And the head cannot say to the feet, "I don't need you!"

—1 Cor. 12:18-21

But God has combined the members of the body and has given greater honor to the parts that lacked it, so that there should be no division in the body, but that its parts should have equal concern for each other. If one part suffers, every part suffers with it; if one part is honored, every part rejoices with it. Now you are the body of Christ, and each one of you is a part of it.

—1 Cor. 12:24-27

Pregnancy loss left me broken. My body and emotions took a beating, but it was still so hard to admit I needed help. The fatigue and confusion made it nearly impossible to find the strength to ask for that help. It felt easier to stay depressed than to have to work at getting better. However, the effort it took to reach out for help was well worth it. Qualified, Bible-believing counselors are a gift.

During that first counseling session, my therapist told me he wouldn't be able to help me until I found myself in a place where it hurt too much to stay where I was. He said this to me because he knew recovering from depression was not something I could heal from passively. I was going to have to work hard at my recovery. I would have to push through the sadness and extreme fatigue to fight for my health and healing.

It did hurt too much to stay where I was, and I did want to heal. I felt vulnerable and understood my counselor was in need of prayer to know how to best help me. I began praying diligently before every session, asking God to facilitate our discussion, and to equip my therapist with the gifts he needed. I prayed he would have wisdom, words of knowledge, and that God would reveal to him what was in my heart and life that needed healing. Here is an example from my prayer journal:

> I am so thankful for my counseling sessions. They have been enlightening to me and incredibly helpful. I pray that you would continue to direct those sessions. Please give him words of knowledge and wisdom to share with me. I pray that he wouldn't teach me things that are not of you, but would facilitate me in discovering what is in my heart that you want me to see. Heal my broken and battered heart.

I encourage anyone who is seeking counseling help to pray for your counselor and your counseling sessions. If you are attending a support group, pray for the leader and for your own ability to discern what will be helpful to you. Pray you will not be deceived, that you will be enlightened, and that every session will be productive. Pray like King David, "Search me, O God, and know my heart; test me and know my anxious thoughts. Point out anything in me that offends you, and lead me along the path of everlasting life" (Ps. 139:23-24 NLT).

My counselor let me know from the beginning he was merely a tour guide. He could point out areas needing work, but I would have to cooperate with the Holy Spirit in that work. Ask God to direct you by His Holy Spirit and give you the strength and courage to work through the issues that led to your spiritual and emotional illness.

WHAT ABOUT MEDICATION?

It appears to be common in Christian circles to oppose the use of medication to treat depression. In an attempt to point people to the true Healer, Christian teachers have condemned the use of antidepressants, requesting that people seek biblical wisdom, prayer, and faith to treat their troubled emotions and bodies.

It is true that our healing will not come from a pill. The pill only treats the symptoms. God is the healer of our hearts and bodies. However, the reality of life is that *sin affects everything*. I saw this in my body's failure to maintain the lives of my babies. Our bodies do not function as they were originally designed to do, but God has equipped us with helpful medical knowledge to deal with this fact.

The decision of whether or not to use antidepressants requires prayerful discernment. The use of this God-given technology is not a sign of spiritual failure. Although my antidepressant could not heal me, it did treat symptoms and allowed me to have more strength to combat depression. I believe God used medication as a tool of relief.

GRIEVING FIRST

With that extra measure of relief provided by the medication, I was better able to focus on the spiritual and emotional aspects of my healing. The first place God led me in dealing with my depression was to grief. This surprised me. I took my medication and went to counseling hoping to be cured and to feel "normal." I didn't expect God to begin by asking me to face grief, sadness, and darkness. His intention was to purge the grief and despair I was holding inside. Holding it in and trying to be spiritually strong, kept the toxins inside. I had to trust Him enough to face the darkness, to cry a lot, and to allow myself to feel pain, instead of continuing on with my plastic smile and the fake response of, "Everything's fine. I'm okay."

My counselor urged me to read the book I mentioned earlier, *A Grace Disguised: How the Soul Grows Through Loss* by Dr. Jerry Sittser.[1] I was amazed to read how similar Dr. Sittser's response to loss was to mine, even though our loss resulted from different circumstances. This book gave me the courage to grieve and allowed me to understand how my soul was growing because of the losses I had endured. Grief must be faced. When it is denied, bad things result. Facing grief is the starting point for healing from the despair.

SHATTERED DREAMS

After I allowed myself to grieve, the next step was to examine how my loss had affected my personal dreams. When I was a little girl, I had an obsession with baby dolls. I had twenty-two of them at one time. All of them slept in bed with me. When my dad tucked me in at night, he had to kiss every one of them goodnight. I insisted that they were *real* babies. I was a child of the 1980's, so when Baby Alive came out, a doll that actually drank water and ate baby food and needed her diapers changed, I had to have one. Baby Alive was on my Christmas wish list for several years. From the beginning, my heart yearned to be a mother in every way.

Later in life when I began making career plans, I had many options open because my grades were very good. My guidance counselor was pushing for an Ivy League school, but I knew in my heart that ultimately the career I wanted most of all was to be a mom and a homemaker. I thought my guidance counselor was going to have a heart attack when I told her of my dream. In her mind, it was a waste of talent. In my mind, it was the achievement of the best in life: family, love, babies.

I chose to teach. It allowed me to work in education, a field I truly loved, put me in contact with kids every day, and the work schedule would benefit a family someday if I couldn't stay home. All of my educational choices and career moves pointed to the ultimate goal of being Mommy.

Not every woman dreams of having a family and children some day, but for many of us, having babies is generated from the core of who we are. Miscarriage can be so painful because it shatters a lifelong and cherished dream. Even if the pregnancy loss occurs after we have already had children, it reaches to the core of our heart—the part of us that longs for a full home and babies to love and to hold. How will we survive if that dream is shattered forever?

One of the areas I had to explore as I was trying to climb out of the pit of despair was my shattered dreams and how they magnified the pain of my losses. All I had planned and hoped for in this life centered around family. I didn't know what to do with myself when faced with the fact that my future might not hold any more pregnancies or babies.

During one counseling session, my therapist asked, "I wonder; do babies equal life to you?" I remember that I felt incredibly resentful and angry at the question, especially coming from a man with four children. I didn't voice my anger, but I left thinking, *What's wrong with wanting babies and a family? Isn't that a good thing? I'm not making an idol out of babies, I'm just sad because my babies died. Isn't that okay?* But as the days went by, the question kept running through my mind.

In this world where sin has affected everything, we are only guaranteed one thing. We are not guaranteed happiness, wealth, health, or even life. We could be hit by a bus as we step off a curb today. My counselor reminded me that we are only guaranteed God Himself and that needs to be enough. It is painful to lay your dreams on an altar and say, "Whom have I in Heaven but you? And earth has nothing I desire besides you. My flesh and my heart may fail, but God is the strength of my heart and my portion forever" (Ps. 73:25-26). When we trust God with our dreams and our lives, we find along with Abraham that He answers, I am "your very great reward" (Gen. 15:1). I need to be seeking life, purpose, and joy within Him. Someday, He may bless me with a successful pregnancy, but that cannot be the defining factor of whether or not I am okay. I had to learn to be okay in Him, regardless of my circumstances. Great blessing and joy will come our way when we can sing "I Surrender All"[2] and really mean it. Elisabeth Elliot says, "Open hands should characterize the soul's attitude toward God- open to receive what He wants to give, open to give back what He wants to take."[3]

DAY BY DAY

Climbing out of the pit of despair is a process. I had to take it day-by-day and moment-by-moment. I was always in a hurry to get done, to be healed, and to be "normal" again. When I'd come home from my counseling appointments and my husband would jokingly ask, "Are you cured yet?" I wanted so badly to say, "Yep, all better!" I wanted to be able to say this, but God does His work at His speed, not mine, and He does it perfectly.

At first, I could not think about the future at all. Each day was enough for me to handle. I was stressed just knowing I had an appointment coming up later in the week. All I could do was make it through to bedtime.

That was actually a pretty healthy way to live. *I'm not guaranteed tomorrow, so I'm just focusing on right now.* It was so freeing not to worry about anything but the one day ahead of me. I began looking at each day and asking, *What does God have for me today? How am I with the Lord? What do I have to praise Him for today? What does He want to do through me today?* Each morning, it was almost as if I was surprised to wake up. I'd think, *Oh, I guess I'm doing this again.*

I started to really enjoy my kids and my home. Joy began seeping back in as I lived day by day. As healing came, my ability to think further forward without pain also increased. At the beginning, every thought of the future was a reminder of how the future would never be what I wanted it to be. Slowly, I could start making plans again. Soon, I found I was enjoying activities I'd given up. Healing was slow, but it wasn't just a Band-Aid over the pain. God dug deep, so that He could really get to and heal the hurt permanently. God doesn't offer quick fixes; He offers permanent fixes.

PAIN IS NOT THE ENEMY

> Consider it wholly joyful, my brethren, whenever you are enveloped in or encounter trials of any sort or fall into various temptations. Be assured and understand that the trial and proving of your faith bring out endurance and steadfastness and patience. But let endurance and steadfastness and patience have full play and do a thorough work, so that you may be [people] perfectly and fully developed [with no defects], lacking in nothing.
>
> —Jas. 1:2-4 AMP

Growing through pain is part of that permanent fix. Pain is not the enemy. It is human nature to avoid pain and to seek pleasure. We all want to be comfortable. We don't want to hurt; yet, we long to have a fruitful life and a character that is more Christ-like.

The refining process that is required to develop us into the person we long to be can be painful, yet often pain leads to beauty. The most beautiful souls I know have suffered great pain. We can laugh as we say to ourselves, *All of this pain and hurt I've been going through is like spiritual cosmetic surgery.*

"Pain is not the enemy" can exhort us during times of hurt. Grief can sweep over you when you are least expecting it. You can't avoid seeing other pregnant women and the raw emotional pain it brings. It's not even jealousy—just a reminder of your loss that you weren't prepared to face. Instead of allowing it to consume you, you can now say, "Yes, this is a painful reminder of what I have lost, but pain is not the enemy."

Pain allows us to participate in the suffering of Christ, to know Him better, to be refined in a way that will make us more like Him. He embodies all we long for: selflessness, holiness, mercy, love, compassion, patience, and grace. Everything we long to be, but cannot be by our own power, He is. The pruning work of the Holy Spirit through pain makes us more beautiful and more effective for the Kingdom. The branch does not bear fruit if it is not pruned.

The pit of depression is a very painful place to be. It can either destroy us or cause us to grow. In the midst of it, we can experience God's hand of grace lifting us out of the pit through the help of other people.

Thankfully, God did not create us to be alone. He designed us to need each other. He has equipped believers with a variety of gifts to edify and bless the body of Christ. Pride can keep us from benefiting from these gifts. Pride says, "Don't let anyone see you weak." If we are suffering, the entire Body of Christ is suffering (see 1 Cor. 12:16). Allow yourself to be helped by the multitude of gifts God has given His people.

Counseling may not be a financial feasibility. There are several ways to find help if you can't afford professional counseling. Search the Christian community in your town. What is available? Ask for prayer from believers. Don't let the lack of finances be an excuse the Enemy uses to keep you defeated. Pray for God to provide the help you need and be open to receive it when it's provided.

The pit of depression is not a place you need to remain in. Not everyone will experience depression as a result of miscarriage, but if you do, there is hope.

Dear Father,

I am in a pit of despair; I do not have the power to get out of on my own. I pray You will "lift me out of the slimy pit, out of the mud and mire, and set my feet on a rock and give me a firm place to stand" (Ps. 40:2). This grief has left my heart broken and battered, but the Bible promises You "heal the brokenhearted and bind up their wounds" (Ps. 147:3). Please do this for me.

Help me to accept my weakness and ask for the help I need. You have set up the Body of Christ to need one another and to help one another. Please point me to believers who are able to help me in my quest for healing. Give them wisdom, discernment, and words of knowledge for me. Protect me from deception while I am vulnerable. "Search me, O God, and know my heart; test me and know my anxious thoughts. Point out anything in me that offends you, and lead me along the path of everlasting life" (Ps. 139:23-24 NLT).

If professional counseling or antidepressants would be beneficial for my healing, I pray You would connect me with the right counselor and doctor to help me with these things. Please protect me from leaning on these alone to heal me. I know they are just tools You have provided for relief, but I must remember You alone are the Great Physician.

Grant me patience for the process of healing before me. Help me not be in a hurry, but to truly take the time necessary to allow You to complete Your work in my heart. It is Your permanent healing I desire.

In Jesus' Name I pray,
Amen

CHAPTER 9

WHERE YOUR TREASURE IS

LOOKING TO HEAVEN

GOD IS SO good. He began preparing me for my miscarriages long before they came. The year before, the women in the Bible study I attended took turns sharing how they became Christians, and what God had done in their lives after that decision. Each week, our study began with a different woman sharing her testimony. Although I was unaware in that moment, God used one of those stories to prepare me for what would happen in my own life.

Mindy was a bubbly, fun person who radiated joy. Her love for Jesus was evident in her eyes and speech. Never in a million years would I have guessed Mindy had suffered any form of tragedy. She was too happy. But as I listened to her testimony, I realized that joy had grown out of tragedy. Her story left a life-changing impact on me.

We passed the Kleenex box around the table as she told us about how she went into preterm labor during her second pregnancy. Her baby girl lived long enough for Mindy and her husband to hold her and sing "Jesus Loves Me" to her. Tears poured down my face as I listened.

How did Mindy survive that? I thought, *That would kill me.*

She continued her testimony proclaiming her love for Jesus and all God had done in her life. I was amazed. How anyone could go through tragedy like that and come away so strong and full of joy was beyond my imagination.

Her testimony persisted in my thoughts late into the evening as I sat down to watch my favorite TV show before bed. That night's ER episode revolved around John Carter, a doctor in the ER, and his pregnant girlfriend. An ultrasound revealed their baby had died, and the rest of the episode followed the delivery of the baby. Grief stricken, these fictional characters represented what it would be like to go through the death of a baby without Christ and without any hope. Unable to withstand the heartache, Carter's girlfriend leaves him alone and completely broken. In their minds, their baby was dead, period. I turned off the TV, struck by the difference between the ER episode and Mindy's story. Comparing them, I saw one grieving with hope, one grieving without it.

Moving on with life, I forgot about those stories until I needed them one year later. Reminded of the contrast between the two stories, I knew who I wanted to be in the long run. But how could I be? In the middle of real grief and heartache, how could I be like Mindy, someone who grew in beauty and love for the Lord instead of becoming consumed or broken?

What did Mindy have that Carter didn't? Hope. The hope of Heaven was a key ingredient in surviving and healing. My babies were in Heaven, and I needed to look up and see the encouragement the Lord had provided me.

Look up and Lift up Your Head!

Now when these things begin to happen, look up and lift up your heads, because your redemption draws near.
—Luke 21:28 NKJV

The idea of eternity has always been tough for me to grasp. The thought of doing anything *forever* overwhelmed me. The fear of the unknown scared me into ignoring what should have been forefront in my mind as a believer in Jesus. It was easier just to ignore it and not really think about it in detail. I acknowledged the existence of Heaven, but spent very little time thinking about it.

Instead, I focused on this timeline. I'm a dreamer. College, a teaching career, getting married, having babies, maybe even writing the great American novel—these were the items on my map for life. Someday, I'd even be a grandmother. My preparation and dreams ran no further.

When I was in the fourth grade, my teacher ended one school day with silent reading. I reached the most exciting part of the book as the bell rang. I continued reading as I walked home from school. Walking a straight line proved to be a challenge as I kept my eye on the book. I can't imagine how ridiculous I must have looked, stumbling along, falling off the curb at times, yet stubbornly refusing to look up from the story to see where I was going.

That trip home from school was symbolic of the way I lived my life—walking along, looking at my feet until the death of my babies knocked me off the sidewalk of life, compelling me to look up. For the first time, death had hit home, and I was required to think about what came next. Longing for hope, God was faithful to provide it. Hope had been available all along, and it was sad that I had lived my life ignoring Heaven and the joy and purpose it brings to this life. For the first time in my life, I longed for Heaven instead of ignoring it.

DON'T BE IGNORANT ABOUT THOSE WHO HAVE FALLEN ASLEEP

> Brothers, we do not want you to be ignorant about those who fall asleep, or to grieve like the rest of men, who have no hope.
> —1 Thess. 4:13

As believers in Jesus, we are supposed to be encouraged by the hope of Heaven, not afraid of it. The Bible speaks of a group of people who also struggled with grief. Questioning the death of their comrades, the Thessalonians were given the same answer in their grief, to be encouraged by the return of Christ and the hope of Heaven.

Unable to visit them, yet concerned for their welfare, the apostle Paul sent his young companion, Timothy, in his place to strengthen and encourage the Thessalonians in their faith. Returning from Thessalonica, Timothy reported they were grieving and confused about what happened to believers in their fellowship who had died before Christ's return. Paul wrote this encouragement to the church in Thessalonica:

> Brothers, we do not want you to be ignorant about those who fall asleep, or to grieve like the rest of men, who have no hope. We believe that Jesus died and rose again and so we believe that God will bring with Jesus those who have fallen asleep in him. According to the Lord's own word, we tell you that we who are still alive, who are left till the coming of the Lord, will certainly not precede those who have fallen asleep. For the Lord himself will come down from Heaven, with a loud command, with the voice of the archangel and with the trumpet call of God, and the dead in Christ will rise first. After that, we who are still alive and are left will be caught up together with them in the clouds to meet the Lord in the air. And so we will be with the Lord forever. Therefore encourage each other with these words.
>
> —1 Thess. 4:13-18

We, along with the believers in Thessalonica, are exhorted to be confident of the home that awaits our loved ones who have died in Christ. We are to look with excitement for that day when Jesus returns and we are reunited with them. Our relationship with our babies is simply interrupted, not ended. If we belong to Jesus, then we are assured by His own word that He will return for us. When He does, He will bring with Him those we long to see that have preceded us. I will meet Jesus in the air and He will reunite me with David, Micah, James, and Sarah. My relationship with them will last an eternity! My heart will be restored. This is a great hope for now!

Hope is not wishing for something to happen. We can wish for a new car, but that is not true hope. Hope is the certainty of something to come. The certainty that our babies await us in Heaven is a healing gift.

OUR BABIES ARE NOT LOST

But someone may ask, "How are the dead raised? With what kind of body will they come?"

—1 Cor. 15:35

So it will be with the resurrection of the dead. The body that is sown is perishable, it is raised imperishable; it is sown in dishonor, it is raised in glory; it is sown in weakness, it is raised in power; it is sown a natural body, it is raised a spiritual body.

—1 Cor. 15:42-44

Death has been swallowed up in victory. Where, O death, is your victory? Where, O death, is your sting!

—1 Cor. 15:54-55

For lack of a better way to label each miscarriage, I've caught myself saying, "When I lost David" or "When I lost Micah, James, or Sarah." It is an easy way to explain the timing of my story, but the truth is I did not lose them. I suffered a pregnancy loss, but my babies are not lost. My babies are eternal beings. They are not lost: they live!

The Bible promises that when we die we are raised with a new, glorified body. I look forward to a body free from the effects of sin and this fallen world. A body that doesn't age. A body that doesn't ache. Paul wrote that our bodies will be in the likeness of Jesus. "And just as we have borne the likeness of the earthly man, so shall we bear the likeness of the man from Heaven" (1 Cor 15:49). After Jesus' resurrection, He walked through walls, yet He was physical. The disciples could touch Him. He ate food. What an amazing thing it will be to have an imperishable body. I long for this for myself, but I am also comforted to know my babies have never known a tummy ache or a headache. They are experiencing the amazing freedom of a body that is not headed for death. They are living in a body that is indestructible and beautiful because it is like that of Christ's.

Is a baby that died before he was born, or that was miscarried at only six weeks gestation, in Heaven? Are we bound for eternity if we were never born? The best resource I know for answering these questions is a book called *I'll Hold You in Heaven* by Jack Hayford. This book has helped countless women following pregnancy loss by laying out the biblical evidence that our miscarried babies exist in Eternity and we will someday hold them in Heaven. The book encouraged me by saying the Bible teaches my babies are not lost; they are "present with the Father" and have "identity, individuality, and deserve to be known for what they are—eternal beings."[1] I recommend this book to anyone who wonders if miscarried babies go to Heaven. The answer is they do!

Do You Believe This?

When Paul wrote to the Thessalonians, he said, "Therefore, encourage each other with these words" (1 Thess. 4:18). There is a choice involved here. We have to choose to believe what the Bible is telling us is true and applicable to our grief.

Jesus reminded his dear friend, Martha, of this after the death of her brother, Lazarus. Jesus comforted her by saying, "I am the resurrection and the life, He who believes in me will live, even though he dies; and whoever lives and believes in me will never die. Do you believe this?" (John 11:25-26).

Reading this question, I heard in my heart, "Do you believe this, Becky? Will you choose to be encouraged and comforted by this wonderful truth, or will you harden your heart to the reality of what I have done on the cross? Do you truly believe I have conquered death? Do you truly believe I am coming back for you? Will you be encouraged?"

I will answer as Martha answered, "Yes, Lord!" Hoping for what we cannot see takes discipline. If I am going to find encouragement from the hope of Heaven, I have to choose to believe Heaven is a reality.

Jesus used Lazarus as an example of what He will do for all of us who have put our faith in Him. He raised Lazarus from the dead, just as He will raise me, just as He will raise my little ones. Satan hoped to kill, steal, and destroy my children and me. Jesus was victorious over Satan, and the grave will not hold all who belong to Him. We are going home.

LOOKING FOR HOME

Set your minds on things above, not on earthly things.
—Col. 3:2

Do not store up for yourselves treasures on earth, where moth and rust destroy, and where thieves break in and steal. But store up for yourselves treasures in Heaven, where moth and rust do not destroy, and where thieves do not break in and steal. For where your treasure is, there your heart will be also.
—Matt. 6:19-21

Each of the four babies I miscarried took a huge piece of me with them when they died. I am closer to Heaven than I was before my losses, because a part of my heart is there now. I long to be there as I have never longed before. Philippians 3:20 reminds me that my "citizenship is in Heaven."

It is one of the beautiful results of these losses. I have treasure waiting for me in Eternity, reminding me to look up and to set my mind on Heaven. This earth has never been my home. There is misery here. My heart is broken by death. My womb is empty. The prince of this world rules with an iron fist. But this world is not my destination. I am Heaven bound. I am closer now then ever before. Romans 13:11 reminds me "the hour has come for you to wake up from your slumber, because our salvation is nearer now than when we first believed."

As I examine my soul, I see how much I have always longed for Heaven. I love beauty. I crave righteousness. In his book, *A Place*

For You, Pastor Jon Courson, says it this way, "You know what you are craving? Heaven. Our hearts are restless, hungering for that which is eternal. There's something in us that knows innately and instinctively that Heaven is not here. We keep looking for it, only to be greatly frustrated."[2]

In his book, *The Journey of Desire,* John Eldredge explains how our tragedies in this life remind us of the beauty that is to come. He says, "Even our troubles and our heartbreaks tell us something about our true destiny. The tragedies that strike us to the core and elicit the cry, 'This isn't the way it was supposed to be!' are also telling the truth—it *isn't* the way it was supposed to be."[3]

The good news is we can look forward to being restored to the way we were meant to be. Restored to the reality of what our hearts' cry is supposed to be. We will experience the beauty, righteousness, and communion with God that our souls crave. Our babies already are.

But does that mean I am destined to despair while I wait for Heaven? Absolutely not! Christ said He came to give us life abundantly. We are broken now. We are torn up, but we can begin to experience a glimmer of Heaven simply by looking for it. Courson says it this way, "If we live for the kingdom of Heaven, life becomes a total joy here and now."[4]

WAIT PATIENTLY

I consider that our present sufferings are not worth comparing with the glory that will be revealed in us.

—Rom. 8:18

For in this hope we were saved. But hope that is seen is no hope at all. Who hopes for what he already has? But if we hope for what we do not yet have, we wait for it patiently.

—Rom. 8:24-25

So we fix our eyes not on what is seen, but on what is unseen. For what is seen is temporary, but what is unseen is eternal.

—2 Cor. 4:18

After experiencing pregnancy loss, we can accept the gift of hope. We must realize we are closer to Heaven than ever before. Even now we can begin to experience the joy of Heaven. We must allow ourselves to be encouraged by the truth of His Word. Pregnancy loss creates deep pain. If, as Paul says in Romans 8:18, this deep pain isn't even "worth comparing with the glory that will be revealed in us," imagine how wonderful Heaven must be! We can wait patiently for this gift. We can choose to grieve with hope, not like those on the television show who revealed how hopeless the world is when they grieved. We hope for what we have not seen because it isn't a fable; it is reality. That hope is healing.

Dear Father,

You have told us to grieve with hope. Show me how to do this. Thank you for providing hope.

Lord, help me to look up, and to set my mind on things above. Please give me an eternal perspective. Thank you that my baby is not lost, but with You. Thank you that I will hold, hug, and kiss my baby and that our relationship is merely interrupted. We will have an eternity to love one another.

Teach my heart the truths of Your Word so I can choose to be encouraged. Thank you that death no longer has victory over those who believe in You!

My pain is so real and deep, yet your Word says it isn't even worth comparing to the glory You have for us. How amazing Heaven must be! Help me to wait patiently.

I pray for the joy that can be mine if I live with Heaven in sight.

In Jesus' Name I pray,
Amen

CHAPTER 10

NOW WHAT?

FACING THE FUTURE

NOT HAVING AN explanation for these losses has been the most difficult part of facing the future. As I write the ending to this book, my pregnancy losses still remain a mystery. There probably will never be a diagnosis or a cure. I often fantasize about a doctor someday saying to me, "We figured out what is wrong! And as long as we do _____ next time, you won't have a problem again." I long for a fix. I have always felt that if I could just understand why it all happened, I could move on and put it behind me.

I still struggle with having to face a future that is different than the one I had planned. How can I have a happy future without another baby? If we try again, how would we stand another loss? How could we do it without living in constant fear? Would another pregnancy loss kill me? Should we give up? What other tragedy could the future hold for us?

The cumulative losses have left me feeling like a runner who is stopped before finishing a race, then told to run in circles to keep warm until the officials can decide where to move the finish line. Pregnancy requires future planning and when the baby is gone, figuring out how to keep going forward feels impossible. It is as if you are stripped of purpose, as if a giant finger in the sky has reached down and pushed pause on the DVD player of life. I didn't know how to jumpstart my life again. I was stuck and the future felt impossible.

JUST DO THE NEXT THING

I met with my pastor's wife, Cathy, the other day for coffee. We talked about my book and some of the things I was writing about. She told me a story about going to a conference and hearing Elisabeth Elliott speak. Elisabeth told the audience that during her own personal times of grief, when people asked her how she was able to cope, she answered she would just do the next thing that needed doing.[1] It is the old one foot in front of the other idea. Instead of being terrified by a future that is too overwhelming, just do the next thing that needs doing. Don't face the entirety of your future. Face today. Face this moment. In reality, it is all we really have.

The day after I had my second D&C procedure, our church held a city-wide women's conference and hosted Elizabeth George as the guest speaker. I had planned on attending the event and was disappointed when I missed it. My church gave me a CD set of the conference as a gift. Her subject for the day was "A Woman after God's Own Heart." As I listened to the CD's, one lesson rose above the rest and stuck with me. She spoke about how easily we can become trapped in the "if-onlies" of life. She encouraged the women attending that day to ask themselves, "What is true about today and what am I going to do about it?"[2]

It struck me how often I am either living in the past pining over the "if-onlies," or living for the future "I'll be happy whens." I often define myself by my goals—by the me I hope to be. However, my purpose didn't die with my babies, and it is not on pause as I wait for another child. My purpose is defined by the answer to this question, *Who does God want me to be today, and what does He want me to do about it?*

As I worked through the difficult task of facing the future without my babies, realizing and applying these truths has been a gift. I now see each day as a picture of life. We are "born" in the morning and "die" at night. I am responsible for the time in between and it is all that I am guaranteed. Each day I am "resurrected" with the grace and new mercies I need for that day. I began asking myself, *How will I live the 'life' I am given today?* I would remind myself, *Today, I am Pat's wife. Today, I am my girls' mom. Today, I am a neighbor. Today, I am Roy and Sally's daughter.* The list went on and as it did, I discovered the answer to jumpstarting my life again: living moment by moment and fulfilling my purpose in the now.

I also had to learn to be content with who I was and what my purpose was for that day. The "if-onlies" and the "I'll be happy whens" had to be replaced with, "I have learned the secret of being content in any and every situation" (Phil. 4:12). The great theologian, C.H. Spurgeon said it this way, "You say, 'If I had a little more, I should be very satisfied.' You make a mistake. If you are not content with what you have, you would not be satisfied if it were doubled."[3]

Lessons from Esther

I also had to trust that God was in control of my future. In May of this year, I was asked to lead a Bible study. The current leader had too much on her plate and needed to resign. When she told me she had chosen Esther as the next study for the group, I was a little nervous because Esther is an awesome story and I was worried it might be a hard one to teach. Some theologians, including Martin Luther, have questioned why this book is even included in the Bible. God is never mentioned by name, and there is no mention of prayer, Heaven, or any other topic you would expect to see in a book of the Bible. I started to wonder, *What are we going to talk about for nine weeks?*

As I studied, I quickly learned that God may appear absent in the book of Esther, however, He is anything *but* absent from this story. In fact, He is a major character. In a sermon on the book of Esther, Jon Courson points out that throughout the book "God is in the shadows, controlling the situation, and governing the circumstances."[4]

I began to relate to this story more than I had anticipated. In fact, my fear of not having enough material for nine weeks proved to be unfounded. Instead of nine weeks to finish the study, it took us five months to finish our study of Esther!

The Jewish people were facing total annihilation. They faced a tremendous crisis, yet in a single day, God in His supposed absence, worked out the circumstances and details to rescue His people. The solution to their horrible situation appeared sudden and full of coincidence, but it wasn't sudden to our sovereign God. It was perfectly timed and perfectly accomplished.

How often God can appear absent from our lives! But He promises He will never leave us nor forsake us and God is faithful to His promises. As we face the future, it can feel as if we have been abandoned, but if you belong to Jesus, you do not face this overwhelming future alone. You face it not only with Him, but in Him.

In Him

Peace to all of you who are in Christ.

—1 Pet. 5:14

When I am raised to life again, you will know that I am in my Father, and you are in me, and I am in you.

—John 14:20 NLT

None of this fazes us because Jesus loves us. I'm absolutely convinced that nothing—nothing living or dead, angelic or demonic, today or tomorrow, high or low, thinkable or unthinkable—absolutely nothing can get between us and God's love because of the way that Jesus our Master has embraced us.

—Rom. 8:31-39 THE MESSAGE

After listening to a Bible study lesson a few years ago, I drew a tiny dot with a circle around it in the margin of my Bible. Above it I wrote the words, "Me, surrounded by God." I didn't know when

I drew it or how much I would be challenged to trust those words; but there is comfort in knowing everything that has reached me has come through God first. It reminds me of superheroes who have powerful force fields around them. "Me, surrounded by God!" Anything that penetrates my force field has to go through God first, who not only loves me, but is by very nature love! (God is love, 1 John 4:8.)

After enduring tragedy, it is common to wonder what may be coming next. It is a great comfort for me to know that all future events must first be filtered through my loving Jesus before they reach me. I know His character and trust His love. It hasn't always been this way. It has been a struggle to come to grips with His love and to trust fully that He loves *me* uniquely and individually. It is my ongoing prayer request to be firmly rooted in His love. Before I can face an unknown future, I need to know deep inside myself that Jesus loves me, accepts me, and has my best interest at heart. It is an essential step to spiritual maturity and strength. "And I pray that you, being rooted and established in love, may have power, together with all the saints, to grasp how wide and long and high and deep is the love of Christ, and to know this love that surpasses knowledge—that you may be filled to the measure of all the fullness of God" (Eph. 3:17-19). If you doubt His love for you, pray that He will reveal it to your heart in a real way.

I love this quote from Adoniram Judson, a missionary to Burma in the early 1880's who suffered much loss during his lifetime, "If I had not felt certain that every additional trial was ordered by infinite love and mercy, I could not have survived my accumulated sufferings."[5] Confidence in God's love is vital for trusting Him for your future.

Soul Suicide

The desire for children, for babies, and for family is a God-given, beautiful, and natural gift. But after the suffering that comes with pregnancy loss, that desire is an easy target. It is painful to want, to consider trying again, and to open yourself up to the possibility of more loss. It becomes almost easier to shut off our hopes and dreams because it hurts too much to want them. It is so hard to want something so much and yet be so terrified of going after it.

In his book, *The Journey of Desire*, John Eldredge explains the human dilemma of being unable to live with our own desire. He calls this dilemma a tragedy that "is increased tenfold when the suicide of soul is committed under the conviction that this is precisely what Christianity recommends. We have never been more mistaken."[6]

Sacrificing your desire to be a mother is not the answer to facing the future. I've seen two negative responses to continual loss. The first is a resignation to "this is just the way it is. God must not want me to have children." The second is to give up because of fear of more loss.

We are called to endure trials, but enduring them is different than resigning ourselves to a depressed, joyless life. Nor is it the stuffing away of our deepest longings. James says that we are to "count it all joy when we fall into various trials" (Js. 1:2 NKJV). Enduring trials includes joy in the midst of the pain. There is hope in this endurance. Jesus set us free to have an abundant life. Christians are uniquely able to find their deepest desires met in the Lord. Don't stop longing for a child just because you think resignation is the Christian thing to do.

It is important to seek God for counsel about what He wants for your family. If in the midst of seeking Him for guidance the desire for children remains, ask Him to fulfill your desires in a way that is in line with His will. Ask Him to give you the ability to endure with joy and hope, not fear and depression. As you surrender your dreams to Him, those dreams may change course and look different than when you began, but the answer will be just right.

TRUSTING GOD TO WRITE OUR LIFE'S STORY

Father, if you are willing, please take this cup of suffering away from me. Yet I want your will to be done, not mine.

—Luke 22:42 NLT

Lord, I believe; help thou mine unbelief.

—Mark 9:24 KJV

All he does is just and good, and all his commandments are trustworthy.

—Ps. 111:7 NLT

God is faithful (reliable, trustworthy, and therefore ever true to His promise, and He can be depended on).

—1 Cor. 1:9 AMP

Some of my favorite books are Jan Karon's series of novels *The Mitford Series*. Set in the small Southern town of Mitford, they tell the story of a lovable, Episcopalian priest, named Father Tim.

I have learned so much from Father Tim, but the most important lesson I have learned from him is his famous "prayer that never fails." Whenever he is counseling someone or trying to figure out a situation, he suggests they pray the prayer that never fails, "Thy will be done."[7]

If we are honest, we can admit we are often afraid of what that "will" might include. It is almost as if we see God in Heaven saying, "Yippee! She finally surrendered. Now I can pour on the really hard stuff!" But we forget God's character. He isn't out to get us. He is out to love us, mold us, shape us, draw us to Himself, and ultimately work out what is best for us individually and for the Kingdom as a whole.

I am able to face the future now because I can pray honestly, "Thy will be done." If praying this prayer terrifies you, list what you are afraid of, confess your unbelief, and ask God to help you to trust Him more. It is a decision you make, but it is God who will give you the ability to do it. This quote from Andrew Murray has encouraged me in my quest for the ability to fully surrender my future, my life, and my dreams:

"Oh, I want to encourage you, and I want you to cast away every fear. Come with that feeble desire. If there is the fear which says—'Oh, my desire is not strong enough. I am not willing for everything that may come. I do not feel bold enough to say I can conquer everything'—I implore you, learn to know and trust your God now. Say, 'My God, I am willing that You should make me willing.'"[8]

Give the Lord your fear, and then ask Him to make you willing and able to surrender to His good will.

AND THEY LIVED HAPPILY EVER AFTER

I kept expecting the happy ending so I could finish this book. I thought for sure the ending would include pictures of our miracle baby. I envisioned photos of our smiling family, holding a newborn, and showing everyone the happy conclusion to our period of sorrow. But as my husband informed me the other day, I'm not writing a fairy tale. I have been writing about real life and real hurts. This book needs to end with a real solution and not, "And they lived happily ever after. The End."

I learned I had to be okay with or without another baby. In order to experience true freedom, I had to come to a point where I could say, "My Jesus is enough." It has been the most painful journey of my lifetime. However, it has also been the most fruitful time of my life. I have learned so much about myself, my blessings, and my God. I would never choose for my babies to die, but I already see great beauty in how God is working and shaping something for good that Satan intended for evil. He is a Master Artist.

Our personal story may yet end in the photos of a miracle baby. But it will not be the subject of those photos that determine my spiritual health. That work is already being accomplished by the masterful work of the Great Physician who saw my wounds and healed them. I am eternally grateful.

As I conclude this book, I am six weeks pregnant for the seventh time. I do not know what the outcome will be, but I have great hope and trust in Jesus. Our heart and home will be full, I have no doubt.

And for you my friend, remember our God is trust*worthy*. Don't forget the worthy part. He has completely earned our trust and demonstrated over and over again that He is worthy.

He is also love. He loves *you* individually, personally, and is intimately involved in your life and in your healing. "How gracious he will be when you cry for help! As soon as he hears, he will answer you" (Isa. 30:19).

I have prayed earnestly for you and will continue to do so. I am fully convinced that as you cling to Him, there will be beauty for your ashes, healing for your grieving heart, and great hope for the future that lies ahead.

> "For I know the plans I have for you," declares the LORD, "plans to prosper you and not to harm you, plans to give you hope and a future."
>
> —Jer. 29:11

APPENDIX A

HELPING A FRIEND WHO HAS

MISCARRIED

10 Practical Ways to Show Your Love

1. Pray, Pray, and Pray Some More

One night after our first miscarriage, my husband and I lay in bed talking about how amazingly tangible the prayers of our family, friends, and even strangers were to us. There was no way to fully express how grateful we felt to be covered in prayer, and we were sure that many would never know how much they had helped us by remembering us in prayer.

It is frustrating to feel that you don't know how to help. You may find yourself saying, "All I can do is pray." Yet faithful prayer for your hurting friend is absolutely the best gift you can give her. Lifting her to God, you are no longer relying on your own ability to help, but can rely on the amazing and abundant resources of God to heal her.

I suggest using this book's Table of Contents as a guide on how to pray specifically for her. The chapter titles help you know some of the challenges that lie ahead for her as she mourns the loss of this child. For example, pray she will draw near to God. Pray she will be protected from spiritual attack. Pray against bitterness, fear, depression, and hopelessness.

Prayer helps you discern how best to be a support and help to your friend. Everyone grieves differently. Only God can give you the wisdom about this specific woman and what will be helpful to her.

Remember, she will be healing from this loss for a long time. Be faithful in your prayers for her even when you think she may not need them any more. You will give her a priceless gift.

2. LET HER GRIEVE

Grieving is a necessary journey that is required for healing. It may be delayed, but it won't be denied. Instead of always trying to cheer her up, allow your friend to grieve, to cry when she needs to, and to know that you acknowledge her loss and the pain she is feeling. Make your words and body language express permission to grieve. Especially if she had an early miscarriage, she may not know it is okay to grieve.

3. BE WISE WITH YOUR WORDS

Reckless words pierce like a sword, but the tongue of the wise brings healing.

—Prov. 12:18

In Chapter 7 of this book, you can read about words that hurt. Pray that you will be the friend who brings healing with your words, not more pain or confusion. Choose every word wisely. Do not offer unsolicited advice. However, don't be afraid to speak. Your friend needs you and your comfort. Be prayerful about the words you write or say to her. If you feel prompted to share something difficult, make sure it is coming from the Holy Spirit and not from your own opinion. If you are unsure, pray instead of speaking. Listen more than you talk. When you need to speak challenging truths to your friend, and you are certain she needs to hear them, speak with grace, humility, and love. Remember that it isn't just about being right. You may be completely right but can cancel out the wisdom you are trying to share when it is delivered from a prideful heart. Seek God's discernment so that your words can be a gift (see Eph. 4:29).

4. BE A GOOD LISTENER

After my first miscarriage, my friend, Jennifer, and I went to see a movie. Afterwards, she drove me home and we sat in her car talking. The conversation started light, but soon moved into how I was doing. Jennifer listened to me, encouraging me to keep going. I didn't realize how much I needed to talk about the details. I let it all out, and I discovered things I was thinking and feeling that I didn't even know were bothering me. I left that car feeling as if a huge load had been lifted off of me. Jennifer didn't need to say a word. She didn't offer any wisdom or try to make me feel better; she just listened, and that was exactly what I needed.

There had been other times when I had felt the need to talk it all out, but had sensed that the other person was resistant. I think many were afraid to let me talk too much because they didn't want me to be sad, or they were afraid they wouldn't know what to say. Others would change the subject or try to cheer me up. Listening to your friend talk it all out when she feels up to it will be a great support to her.

5. UNDERSTAND WHEN SHE DOESN'T WANT TO TALK

Although I just said to be a good listener to your friend, it is also important to remember you can't force the issue. There will be times, especially in the beginning, when she has no desire to talk even to her best friends.

The telephone can be so hard to answer when you are grieving. I let the answering machine answer a lot. The messages people left were a huge blessing, so I am not suggesting that you should be afraid to call, just be understanding if she doesn't answer or doesn't return your call any time soon.

6. SHOW UP WITH DINNER

Bringing meals is a practical way to show your love and support. That first night after I returned from the doctor's office with the bad news, my friend, Daiquiri, showed up at the door with Costco lasagna and a batch of cookies, hugged me, told me she loved me, and left. She didn't call to see if I needed it, she just showed up with dinner. It was a perfect gesture and just what I needed that night. My mind was so numb, trying to figure out what to cook for dinner would have been impossible. Many friends brought meals over the course of our losses. By bringing dinner, they showed their love for us in a way we appreciated. We felt loved and taken care of by our friends and family.

7. GIVE THE GIFT OF MUSIC

The night before I went to the hospital to deliver the first baby we lost, my friend, Jeanine, came over to the house with a worship CD. She had been through the same experience a few years earlier, and recommended that I bring a CD player and some instrumental worship music. She said, "It is going to be a long day and it will help to have this playing in the background."

I can't express what a comfort it was to have the music playing throughout that ordeal. There was an unexplainable peace in the delivery room as the music played. It reminded me that Jesus was near.

When I went home, I knew that I needed to draw near to God, but my mind was consumed with the grief. I tried to read the Bible and other Christian books, but I couldn't concentrate. Eventually, I was able to read again and was touched by the words of many books. However, in the beginning, the only thing that could get through to me was music. I kept it playing all the time. The lyrics were often the sermons I needed.

If you are looking for a gift to give your friend, consider giving the gift of Christian music. God used different songs to teach me different things and to offer comfort in amazing ways.

8. ACKNOWLEDGE THE BABY

Even now, it touches my heart when my friends and family refer to my babies by their names. It has been awhile, but they continue to remember.

Many women fear their babies will be forgotten. By acknowledging the baby, not just the loss, you reassure her that the baby's life wasn't in vain and won't be forgotten.

Helping your friend to have a memorial of some kind is helpful. It might be in the form of planting a tree or by giving her a special keepsake necklace or ring. It can be anything that lets her know, even if she lost the baby early in pregnancy, you care about the life lost and acknowledge how much that life meant to her.

9. REMEMBER HER DUE DATE

I was shocked when I got a phone call from my friend, Kristin, on October 10, 2005. She said, "I was just thinking about this being your due date, and I wondered if it would be a tough day for you. I just wanted to make sure you were doing okay."

I had watched the calendar and anticipated the day coming, but I fully expected to be the only one who realized its significance. It touched me so much to have a friend remember.

You can mark your calendar as a reminder and send a card, take your friend out for coffee, or just call her on the phone like Kristin did. It's the remembering that matters.

10. DON'T BE AFRAID TO REACH OUT TO HER

The most important thing to remember is to be there. Don't be an absent friend because of fear. It is easy to want to pull away from her pain. Pray for the wisdom and discernment you need and then stick around and be her friend. You may say and do the wrong things. Just ask for forgiveness from her and continue to be there for her. Pulling away will hurt her worse than any mistake you can make. Forgive her if she hurts you in her process of grieving. Sometimes the people we love the most are the ones we hurt the most. She may be jealous or bitter or just trying to deal with everything and needs your grace and forgiveness. Walk with her for the long-term process of healing and you will be a true friend.

DO YOU KNOW THE HEALER OF

BROKEN HEARTS?

PERHAPS AS YOU'VE read this book wondered if the hope and healing promised throughout these pages are really available to you personally. Maybe you read the chapter on Heaven and aren't even sure if you will be spending eternity there. It is possible the spiritual aspects of this book have left you with more questions than answers.

In my conversations with women going through pregnancy loss many express feelings of helplessness, hopelessness, and brokenness they don't know how to handle. Many are ready to explore spirituality for the first time in their lives. If this is you, I want you to know I have earnestly prayed for you. I started praying for you even before I began to write the first word of this book. I prayed for you every time I sat down to type at my computer. I beseeched God to allow my words to reach your heart and point you to the only true source of healing and hope available: Jesus.

Often in times of brokenness people are finally able to hear God's voice calling them. Their pride isn't in the way anymore. The brokenness they feel is evidence of their need for Him. If this is you, don't ignore His voice. He is wooing you, desiring to heal you completely. Jesus said He "stands at the door and knocks." He wants to begin with healing your soul. Don't go back to a life void of hope. Open the door and let Him in.

The first step is humility. You need to admit your need for a Savior. You may be able to see now how little control you really have over your life and destiny and recognize your inability to fix your heartache and areas of sin in your life. The good news is, "The sacrifices of God are a broken spirit; a broken and contrite heart, O God, you will not despise" (Ps. 51:17).

When you come to Him in your brokenness, acknowledging your sin and your need for Him, He will not despise you. He will forgive you and heal you. When you place your faith in Jesus, He will engrave your name in the palms of His hands. He will write your name in the Book of Life. You won't have to wonder if you'll spend eternity in Heaven or if you will ever see your babies. You will know.

If you are ready to turn your life over to Him, go to Him in prayer. You don't need fancy words. You do not need to get yourself ready, cleaned up, or get religion first. Just throw yourself at His feet and tell Him you need Him. Ask for and accept His forgiveness. Give up control and allow Him to be Lord of your life. Put your faith in Him and begin to get to know the Lover of Your Soul.

If you have made this decision, please tell me about it. You can contact me at beckyavella@gmail.com

Also, don't try to do this on your own. Seek out a Bible believing and teaching church. Find small groups to get involved in like women's Bible studies, and start learning more about Jesus and this relationship you've just entered into.

I am so excited about the hope you will find and the healing that awaits!

Love,
Becky

ENDNOTES

Chapter 2

1. C.S. Lewis, *The Magician's Nephew* (Harper Collins, 1983), p. 87.

2. Francisco, Don. "Willing to Heal" Lyrics. The Power. Don Francisco EMI, 1987. Used by permission.

Chapter 3

1. Sittser, Jerry. *A Grace Disguised: How the Soul Grows Through Loss* (Zondervan, 1995), p. 29.

Chapter 4

1. Ten Boom, Corrie. *The Hiding Place* (Chosen, 2007), pgs. 196-197.

Chapter 5

1. Grant, Natalie. "Held" Lyrics. *Awaken*. WEIMARRHYMES PUBLISHNG INC.2005. (Songwriter: Wells, Christa)

2. Dictionary.com <http://dictionary.reference.com/browse/defile>

3. Chapman, Steven Curtis. "God is God" Lyrics. Declaration. Sparrow, 2001.

Chapter 6

1. White, John. *The Fight*. (InterVarsity Press, 1976), p. 217.

2. Anderson, Neil T. *The Bondage Breaker*. (Harvest House, 1990), p. 23.

3. McGee, Robert S. *The Search for Significance*. (W. Publishing Group, 2003), pgs. 141-151.

4. Sherman, Dean. *Spiritual Warfare for Every Christian*. (YWAM Publishing, 1990), p. 168.

Chapter 7

1. Kincaid, Jorie. *Adopting for Good*. (InterVarsity Press, 1997), p. 44.

Chapter 8

1. Sittser, Jerry. *A Grace Disguised: How the Soul Grows Through Loss*. (Zondervan, 1995).

2. I Surrender All

3. Elliot, Elisabeth, emailed devotion, exact source unknown

Chapter 9

1. Hayford, Jack. *I'll Hold You in Heaven*. (Regal, 1990), p. 66.

2. Courson, Jon. *A Place For You*. (Calvary Chapel Publishing, 2003), p. 133.

3. Eldredge, John. *The Journey of Desire*. (Thomas Nelson, 2000) p. 12.

4. Ibid.

Chapter 10

1. Elliot, Elisabeth, source unknown

2. George, Elizabeth. 2006 Treasure Valley Women's Conference, January 21, 2006, Boise, ID

3. Spurgeon, C.H., source unknown

4. Courson, Jon. Sermon, May 21, 1986 and November 17, 2002. (http://www.joncourson.com)

5. Judson, Adoniram, source unknown

6. Eldredge, John. *The Journey of Desire.* (Thomas Nelson, 2000), pg. 30.

7. Karon, Jan. Mitford Series. (Penguin Books)

8. Murray, Andrew. *Absolute Surrender.* (Whitaker House, 1981), pgs. 11-12.

Join the Conversation

#AndThenYouWereGone
You can connect with the author on Twitter: @BeckyAvella or
on Facebook under the book's title:
And Then You Were Gone: Restoring a Broken Heart After
Pregnancy Loss.

Remember that online reviews are the best gift you can give back
to your favorite authors. If you enjoyed *And Then You Were
Gone*, would you consider leaving a review on Amazon.com,
Goodreads, or any other online source?
Thank you!

Made in the USA
Las Vegas, NV
23 August 2022

53872798R00069